The Small Museum Toolkit, Book 4

About the Series

The American Association for State and Local History Book Series publishes technical and professional information for those who practice and support history, and addresses issues critical to the field of state and local history. To submit a proposal or manuscript to the series, please request proposal guidelines from AASLH headquarters: AASLH Book Series, 1717 Church St., Nashville, Tennessee 37203. Telephone: (615) 320-3203. Fax: (615) 327-9013. Website: www.aaslh.org.

About the Organization

The American Association for State and Local History (AASLH), a national history organization headquartered in Nashville, TN, provides leadership, service, and support for its members, who preserve and interpret state and local history in order to make the past more meaningful in American society. AASLH is a membership association representing history organizations and the professionals who work in them. AASLH members are leaders in preserving, researching, and interpreting traces of the American past to connect the people, thoughts, and events of yesterday with the creative memories and abiding concerns of people, communities, and our nation today. In addition to sponsorship of this book series, the Association publishes the periodical *History News*, a newsletter, technical leaflets and reports, and other materials; confers prizes and awards in recognition of outstanding achievement in the field; and supports a broad education program and other activities designed to help members work more effectively. To join the organization, go to www.aaslh.org or contact Membership Services, AASLH, 1717 Church St., Nashville, TN 37203.

The Small Museum Toolkit, Book 4

Reaching and Responding to the Audience

Edited by
Cinnamon Catlin-Legutko
and Stacy Klingler

ALTAMIRA
PRESS

A division of
ROWMAN & LITTLEFIELD PUBLISHERS, INC.
Lanham • New York • Toronto • Plymouth, UK

Published by AltaMira Press
A division of Rowman & Littlefield Publishers, Inc.
A wholly owned subsidary of The Rowman & Littlefield Publishing Group, Inc.
4501 Forbes Boulevard, Suite 200, Lanham, Maryland 20706
http://www.altamirapress.com

Estover Road, Plymouth PL6 7PY, United Kingdom

British Library Cataloguing in Publication Information Available

Library of Congress Cataloging-in-Publication Data

The small museum toolkit. Book 4, Reaching and responding to the audience / edited by Cinnamon Catlin-Legutko and Stacy Klingler.
    p. cm. — (American Association for State and Local History book series)
    Includes bibliographical references and index.
    ISBN 978-0-7591-1951-2 (cloth : alk. paper) — ISBN 978-0-7591-1338-1 (pbk. : alk. paper) — ISBN 978-0-7591-1345-9 (electronic)
    1. Small museums—Public relations. 2. Communication in museums. I. Catlin-Legutko, Cinnamon. II. Klingler, Stacy, 1976– III. Title. IV. Title: Reaching and responding to the audience.
    AM124.S63 2012
    069.1—dc23   2011028449

∞™ The paper used in this publication meets the minimum requirements of American National Standard for Information Sciences—Permanence of Paper for Printed Library Materials, ANSI/NISO Z39.48-1992.

Printed in the United States of America

CONTENTS

EDITORS' NOTE

S mall museums are faced with the enormous task of matching the responsibilities of a large museum—planning strategically, securing and managing
human and financial resources, providing stewardship of collections (including historic buildings) as well as excellent exhibitions, programs, and publications, and responding to changing community and visitor needs—all with
more limited human and financial resources. Small museum staff (paid or unpaid) often fulfill key responsibilities outside their area of expertise or training.

We recognize that small museum staff lack time more than anything. To
help you in the trenches, we offer this quick reference, written with your working environment in mind, to make the process of becoming a sustainable, valued
institution less overwhelming.

The Small Museum Toolkit is designed as a single collection of short, readable books that provides the starting point for realizing key responsibilities in
museum work. Each book stands alone, but as a collection they represent a
single resource to jump-start the process of pursing best practices and meeting
museum standards.

If you are new to working in museums, you may want to read the entire
series to get the lay of the land—an overview of what issues you should be
aware of and where you can find resources for more information. If you have
some museum training but are now responsible for more elements of museum
operations than in your previous position, you may start with just the books or
chapters covering unfamiliar territory. (You might be wishing you had taken a
class in fundraising right about now!) As you prepare to tackle new challenges,
we hope that you will refer back to a chapter to orient yourself.

While any chapter can be helpful if read in isolation, we suggest that you
start with the first book, *Leadership, Mission, and Governance*, and look at the
issues of mission, planning, and assessment. You will find that almost every
chapter asks you to consider its subject in light of your mission and make decisions based on it. As you begin to feel overwhelmed by all the possible opportunities and challenges you face, assessment and planning will help you focus

your scarce resources strategically—where you need them the most and where they can produce the biggest impact on your organization. And this book offers tips for good governance—defining the role of a trustee and managing the director-trustee relationship. Understanding this relationship from the outset will prevent many headaches down the road.

Financial Resource Development and Management offers you direction about how to raise and manage money and stay within your legal boundaries as a nonprofit. How to manage resources, human and inanimate, effectively and efficiently is discussed in *Organizational Management. Reaching and Responding to the Audience* encourages you to examine your museum audiences and make them comfortable, program to their needs and interests, and spread the word about your good work.

The remaining two books explore the museum foundational concepts of interpretation and stewardship in a small museum setting. *Interpretation: Education, Programs, and Exhibits* considers researching and designing exhibits and best practices for sharing the stories with your audiences. *Stewardship: Collections and Historic Preservation* rounds out the six-book series with an in-depth look at collections care, management, and planning.

We would like to thank the staff at the American Association for State and Local History and AltaMira Press, our families, and our colleagues for encouraging us to pursue this project. You have tirelessly offered your support, and we are incredibly grateful.

There is little reward for writing in service to the museum field—and even less time to do it when you work in a small museum. The contributors to this series generously carved time out of their work and personal lives to share with you their perspectives and lessons learned from years of experience. While not all of them currently hang their hats in small museums, every one of them has worked with or for a small museum and values the incredible work small museums accomplish every day. We offer each and every one of them more appreciation than we can put into words.

We hope that this series makes your lives—as small museum directors, board members, and paid and unpaid staff members—just a little bit easier. We hope that we have gathered helpful perspectives and pointed you in the direction of useful resources.

And when you are faced with a minor annoyance, a major disaster, or just one too many surprises, remember why you do this important work and that you are not alone.

It takes a very special kind of person to endure and enjoy this profession for a lifetime. Not a day passes in which I do not learn something, or find something, or teach something, or preserve something, or help someone.

—Unknown author

Keep up the good work!

Cinnamon Catlin-Legutko
Stacy Lynn Klingler
Editors

PREFACE

I have a confession to make. Until I got to the American Association for State and Local History (AASLH), I never truly understood what it was to work in a small museum. Sure, I had been around them, visited them, talked to my peers who worked in them both as paid and unpaid (read: volunteer) staff, and appreciated the role they play in the historical narrative and in communities. But I never *got it* until I got to AASLH.

So what have I learned? First and foremost, small museums are the bedrock of the American museum profession. You will not find museums the size of the Smithsonian or historic sites like Gettysburg in every American community, but you will often find a small museum, sometimes more than one. While we in the historical profession talk often about how we are the keepers of the American past, and we are, those who work in the smaller institutions are truly minders of our nation's patrimony and heritage. They care for the objects and history of communities throughout the country, stories that would probably be lost without that care. Quite simply, without small museums, our knowledge of the past, our historical narrative, would be incomplete.

The second thing I have learned, and been truly humbled by, is the passion and dedication small museum professionals and volunteers have for their craft. You will rarely hear small museum professionals complaining about a lack of resources—that is just part and parcel of the task at hand. Instead of attacking a challenge with reasons for why something cannot be done, they redirect their thoughts to how it can be done within the parameters provided. So, small museum professionals are equally comfortable with answering the phone, giving a tour, processing collections, and plunging the occasional toilet (the latter falling into the "other duties as assigned" category in a job description).

And amid all that, small museum professionals keep a great sense of humor. At several gatherings of small museum folks over the years, we have had fun with a game we call "You Know You Work in a Small Museum If . . ." Responses ranged from "A staff meeting consists of all staff members turning around in their office chairs at the same time" to "You're the director, but if you're the first one to work after a snowstorm, you get to shovel the sidewalk and plow the parking lot." But my absolute favorite was "When you walk through the gallery and hear a guest say, 'The staff should really do . . .' and you think, Hey, *I'm* my staff!"

At one time, as Steve Friesen of the Buffalo Bill Museum and Grave notes in chapter 2 of Book 1 of this series, the term *small museum* was used as a pejorative. Small museums were underfunded, under-resourced, and poorly managed. "If they weren't," the thinking went, "they'd be large museums, right?" Wrong. Being small does not mean you aspire to be big or that the institution is small because it is doing something wrong. Smallness has more to do with a spirit and dedication to a certain niche of history, a community, a person, a subject.

I believe the field has moved beyond that prejudice, and small museums are now celebrated. At AASLH we often discuss how much larger museums can learn from smaller institutions about how to serve as effective stewards of their resources and to engage their communities in a deep, meaningful way. There is much to learn from small museums, and our peers and colleagues at those institutions are ever willing to share.

Along this line, I have always found that one of the best things about the museum profession in general is how open it is with regard to sharing ideas and processes and just offering support. In no corner of the field is this more evident than in the world of small museums. Small museum professionals are founts of wisdom and expertise, and every small museum session, luncheon, or affinity event I have been to has been packed, and discussion has been stimulating and often inspiring. In fact, discussion often spills out into the hallways after the formal session has concluded.

But the work I know best is that of the AASLH Small Museums Committee. The editors of this series, Cinnamon Catlin-Legutko and Stacy Klingler, are, respectively, the founding and current chairs of this committee. Under their leadership, a team of small museum folks has completed a set of ambitious goals, including gathering a variety of research and developing a small museum needs assessment, presenting sessions at conferences throughout the country, and raising money for scholarships to send peers to the AASLH annual meeting each year. It is this last item I want to highlight as it gives the clearest example of the love and commitment those in small museums have for each other.

In my view, the fact that the Small Museums Committee successfully organizes an annual fundraising campaign is commendable. The fact that it routinely raises money to send *two* people to the meeting (and four people in some years) is truly remarkable. This is indicative of the passion and dedication small museum professionals feel toward the cause of small museums and toward their colleagues. Let's face it, history professionals are not at the top of the salary food chain. (I always note this whenever I speak to history classes about a career in public history. "If you choose this career, you are going to love what you do; you are going to be making a difference in your community. But you are also taking a vow of poverty. No one goes into the history field to get rich.") And while donors to this fund are not all from small museums, small museum professionals are a large part of the pool, giving as generously as anyone. I am so heartened each year as we raise this money.

So, what does all this have to do with the book in your hands? I would say a lot. First, the contributors are small museum professionals or aficionados themselves. They are dedicated to the craft in the small museum environment and know firsthand its needs and challenges. In addition, they have been involved with, and led national discussions on, these issues. They are passionate about the cause of small museums, and they have organized and written a book (and series) that offers a variety of voices and contexts while speaking to the needs as articulated. The thirty-plus contributors to this series offer a wealth of experience and expertise in dealing with the complex nature of running a small museum, in preserving traces of the American past for future generations, often on a shoestring budget and with limited resources. It is a lesson we can all learn. And it is a lesson well articulated here.

Whether you are a seasoned small museum professional, a newly minted executive director, or a museum studies or public history student, it is my hope that this book series will give you the tools you need to succeed in your job. I also hope that you will continue to carry the torch for small museums in your community and in the larger museum field. The field needs your passion and expertise, and the role you fill in your community is critical.

Bob Beatty
Vice President, AASLH

CHAPTER ONE
START SPREADING THE NEWS: MARKETING AND COMMUNICATION
Kara Edie

Resources of almost every type are usually constrained in the small museum world: funds, time, space, and manpower are at a premium and often stretched to the limit in order to make the most of what is available. In this atmosphere, promotion and communication may seem like an afterthought, something that is attended to only after the weighty business of collection, funding, and administration is completed. Many times, marketing seems to be at cross-purposes with the rest of museum work: When a museum's mission is centered on the preservation of artifacts, inviting the public to arrive en masse amid fragile collections may feel dangerous.

Despite its reputation, marketing underpins and supports almost every other objective in a small museum, and investing time and attention to a marketing strategy pays dividends throughout an institution.

Imagine the difficulties of fundraising, for example, with no way of communicating with prospective benefactors. Reaching students with educational programming is almost impossible without their teachers' awareness that the resource is available. Attracting quality employees and volunteers becomes futile when the right candidates have no idea that a need exists. Far from afterthoughts, marketing and communication need to form important parts of every museum's long-range plan.

"No donor will pay you money before they pay you attention. There is no denying that awareness is the absolute first step in all fundraising activity."

—Amy Stark, Stark Reality Enterprises, Inc.[1]

Marketing, in its most general sense, is the art of communicating effectively with an audience. In contrast to sales, which exclusively uses persuasive tactics to convince an audience to commit to a purchase, marketing concerns itself not only with selling but also with building awareness, educating, updating information, and influencing opinions. Marketing is the science of not only attracting an audience but also developing a relationship with that audience and nurturing that relationship to the benefit of both the audience and the organization. Marketing methods are almost innumerable, from press releases and brochures to websites, billboards, social media, and word of mouth. In a small museum, so many options may seem overwhelming—and overly expensive.

Fortunately, especially in the economic climate of the last few years, many of the most effective marketing strategies entail low or no costs and are easy to implement in cultural organizations of any size. What follows is a comprehensive guide on how to design a workable marketing plan and implement the most productive communication strategies in order to reap the highest rewards from your museum's already stretched resources.

Know Your Audience

Getting the word out to your community about your museum's news and needs is made much easier with the help of an organized marketing plan. With thoughtful analysis of your audience, your current marketing efforts, your organization's marketing budget, and your proposed evaluation methods, you can begin promoting your museum much more effectively than if you were simply to begin issuing press releases. By taking time to plan early in your efforts, you can ensure that the marketing initiatives you carry out have the greatest impact with your audience.

Defining your museum's target audience is the logical first step in any marketing plan, and this may seem like an easy task: just look to the community outside the doors of your building and construct a plan that appeals specifically to the people who live and work there. Analyzing your community is a great start, but remember, in these highly connected times, your museum's target market is likely much greater than the people in your geographical area.

Start by evaluating your neighborhood. Recent census figures can give you updated information on the number, gender, ethnicity, and background of the people who live in your area. These are the people who are directly affected by most of your museum's local initiatives, like educational programming and special events. Depending on your institution's governance, these households may also be helping to fund your work with their tax dollars. It is crucial to maintain clear channels of communication within your community.

Next, look at your museum's current visitors or the visitors to other cultural attractions in your area. Frequently, you will find that more of your visitors come from outside your immediate community, as people are more likely to visit museums and other attractions while traveling. Gather information on the wider region surrounding your community—neighboring states or areas where many of your visitors may originate. This will serve as a map to areas where you may want to invest more of your marketing attention.

Indentify your affinity groups. Regardless of your museum's location, people will be interested in learning about, visiting, and supporting your institution if it revolves around something they find fascinating. My organization, the General Lew Wallace Study & Museum in Crawfordsville, Indiana, focuses on the life and legacy of Lew Wallace, a Civil War major general who went on to write *Ben-Hur*, one of the best-selling novels of the nineteenth century. Wallace was also a Renaissance man, dabbling in painting, sculpting, violin making, and architecture. He was a public servant, foreign ambassador, supporter of women's suffrage, and patented inventor. Our museum is structured around Wallace's beautiful study

TEXTBOX 1.1

EXAMPLE AFFINITY GROUPS

- Fans of historical eras, milestones, or figures: the Roaring Twenties, the American Revolution, Dr. Martin Luther King Jr.
- Devotees of a particular art form or artist: Baroque, plein air watercolor, Pablo Picasso, Salvador Dalí
- Movie buffs or fans of particular genres: *Gone With the Wind, The Wizard of Oz*, sword-and-sandal epics, romantic comedies
- Members of professions: law enforcement officers, farmers, chefs
- People with religious affiliations
- Members of genealogical groups: ancestors of a particular family or descendants from a common geographical location
- Members of military groups: active members or veterans, children of veterans
- Practitioners of hobbies: model train builders, ham radio operators, woodworkers
- People with special interests: lovers of Adirondack architecture, Japanese water gardens, or cha-cha dancing
- Sports aficionados: Chicago Bears fans, downhill skiers, bow hunters

building, a unique sanctuary designed by the general himself, the likes of which cannot be seen anywhere else in the world. Our affinity groups range from Civil War history buffs (of which there are many, as the American Civil War is one of the most widely discussed military conflicts in the world) to literature devotees, to architecture aficionados, to fans of the motion picture versions of *Ben-Hur*. Each of these groups represents an opportunity to attract and communicate with prospective supporters. Your institution's central theme or figure certainly may attract a narrower range of interests, but for almost every subject that exists, be it trains, telegraphy, or Tinkertoys, there lies an interested group of people just waiting to learn more through your organization. (See textbox 1.1 for more examples.)

Discover and Cultivate Customer Evangelists

Affinity groups are the most fertile ground in which to find those rare and valuable supporters called customer evangelists. According to marketing experts Ben McConnell and Jackie Huba, the best indicator of growth is whether a customer would recommend a company's products or services to a friend.[2] An evangelist is a word-of-mouth referral taken to its extreme: an individual so dedicated to your brand that he devotes himself to learning all he can about your organization and spreading your mission to others. While most successful organizations have strong advocates that have helped them to thrive, the rate of customer evangelism has boomed in the last decade, due to technological advances that allow almost anyone with a computer and an Internet connection to share their opinions with an enormous number of people.

Passionate customer loyalists have spurred discussion, ignited debate, and drawn attention to their preferred products and services for years—in many cases, far more than companies have done themselves. In years past, Chevrolet and Ford motor companies both saw their most ardent supporters willingly influencing others as to why their favorite automaker had the best cars. More recently, Apple and Microsoft finally began to reflect the opinions of their most driven computer customers with their respective "I'm a Mac" and "I'm a PC" advertising campaigns. Slogans have been developed around specific brands ("I'm a Bud man," for example, or "It's a Jeep thing, you wouldn't understand"), most of which were coined by customer evangelists.

With the tremendous popularity of the Internet, customer evangelists' influence can be felt across the globe. With just a blog and a passionate opinion, one or a few individuals can reach millions with their messages, good or bad, about specific companies or products. LEGO fans are a classic example. Adult LEGO enthusiasts (or ALEs) began to gather on the Internet in online communities dedicated to their particular interests, such as LEGO sets in *Star Wars*, medieval castle, space, train, or robotic themes. These brand loyalists grew exponentially in number throughout the world, organizing real-world events and conferences where enthusiasts could get together and share new building designs and methods. The enthusiasm of these grassroots groups far surpassed any marketing initiatives that the corporate LEGO Group launched itself. Soon after witnessing this incredible fan support, the LEGO Group embraced its customer evangelists, even soliciting input on upcoming LEGO set designs from the most fervent devotees.

That kind of power can also be brought to cultural institutions through customer evangelists. Museums represent a vast storehouse of stories and artifacts that carry enormous importance in an era where information is king. People touched by your collection and inspired by your mission can, through the simple power of word of mouth, help you share your organization's stories with the rest of this incredibly connected world.

Customer evangelists are easy to spot within your organization and online. Just as you would reward a volunteer who goes above and beyond museum membership to enhance your organization, you can also reward customer loyalists who help your museum grow and prosper by giving them perks such as sneak previews of exhibits, interesting new information about your museum or central figure, or even frequent-shopper discounts at the museum gift shop. Sometimes rewarding customer loyalists takes a mere few clicks if you use Facebook or Twitter to funnel new tidbits of information to an established, receptive audience that is always willing to share what they have learned with their friends.

Competitors and Partners: Analyzing the Market

When planning marketing strategy, it is important to gauge your market: the community around you, including your neighbors and your competitors. It is unlikely that your cultural institution is the only thing of interest to be found in your community. You may have three other museums within a mile of your own (as is the case with the General Lew Wallace Study & Museum), or your museum may be the only cultural organization amid miles of shopping malls, golf courses, theme parks, or other attractions. Every market is different, and each presents its own advantages and challenges. No matter what your market consists of, you should take all venues in your area that attract travelers into account as you construct your marketing plan.

As you list neighboring museums in your plan, do you consider them competitors or potential partners? Certainly they compete with your museum for the cultural tourism audience, but in many cases it works more to the benefit of each organization if you work together rather than competing against one another. Even museums that do not share a common mission or theme can join forces in order to bring cultural travelers to the area. Since many travelers visit several attractions over a single stay, every initiative that draws more tourists to your area can be mutually beneficial.

5

Combining talents also helps to save resources, especially for cultural organizations with very limited marketing budgets. Large-scale advertising like billboards or television spots are often prohibitively expensive for a single nonprofit organization, but sharing the space with other similar groups garners the same wide exposure for a fraction of the price.

Even public relations initiatives that cost little or nothing at all can be made more attractive by working with other museums. Our organization works with our three neighboring museums to promote special events in which we all take part. This makes a much bigger story to pitch to local journalists than if the four of us were to sponsor smaller, separate events. Local newspapers and radio and television stations are more likely to pick up our story, and visitors interested in seeing one of our museums might decide to make a day of it and visit others.

What if your main competitors are not museums, nonprofit organizations, or cultural attractions at all? A savvy museum marketer will capitalize on the willingness of almost any organization to work cooperatively with a quality cultural organization. Museums are great for the community, and a vibrant cultural scene in your area benefits local businesses as well as partner museums. Venues like shopping centers, restaurants, theaters, and hotels can realize added value for themselves (and drive traffic to your door) by offering free museum admission to their customers. In the dynamic world of cultural tourism, you will find that by keeping your marketing plan open to possibilities, you will encounter far more potential partners than competitors.

TEXTBOX 1.2

POTENTIAL PARTNERS

- Colleges and universities
- Senior-living centers
- Elementary and secondary schools
- Tour companies
- Living history reenactment groups
- Girl and Boy Scouts
- Service groups
- Fraternal organizations and sororities
- Veterans' associations
- 4-H clubs
- Garden clubs

Speaking of partners, many established organizations in your area focus on assisting in the promotion of your community, including your museum. Convention and Visitors Bureaus (CVBs) are integral parts of the communities they serve and they will be among your most powerful advocates as a cultural attraction. It is the mission of local CVBs to bring visitors to your area and to extol the benefits of your community to business and personal travelers alike. Indeed, most CVBs spend almost half of their budget on sales and marketing efforts, especially advertising in the media.[3] Since the majority of CVBs are independent nonprofits funded through state and local tourism funds and hotel and restaurant taxes, your museum pays little to nothing for top-quality, high-volume promotion. Make the most of your partnership with your local CVB by supplying it with seasonal event schedules, annually updated photos, printed marketing materials for distribution, and museum-branded items they can sell in their visitor centers (if they feature retail stores).

Another valuable source of marketing assistance can be found through your local and state historical societies. Like your museum, historical societies across the country are in the business of preserving artifacts and interpreting stories from the past that enrich our lives. In addition to the wealth of nonmarketing support available to partner museums, like collections care assistance and grant funding, historical societies can also connect your museum to their extensive membership to help you communicate with like-minded individuals about subjects that interest them. Networking with large audiences interested in local history can tap into previously undiscovered stores of new visitors, donors, and perhaps budding customer evangelists.

Every state in the country has a state tourism office, as do most U.S. territories and hundreds of countries around the world. Partnerships with state tourism offices usually manifest tremendous results, as tourism offices spend millions of dollars every year to advertise both their area's crown jewels and its more hidden gems. Most tourism bureaus publish annual information about statewide attractions as well as guides to shopping, lodging, golf, festivals, and special-interest tours like wine-country drives and historic trails. Tourism websites, like VisitCalifornia.com and VermontVacation.com, are usually run by state tourism commissions, attracting millions of vacation-minded travelers. In addition, state tourism offices organize conferences and special events where local organizations from throughout the state can showcase their attractions to visiting travel writers, group-tour organizers, and developers in the hopes of gaining even wider exposure.

Most state-run tourism marketing initiatives cost money, sometimes a significant amount, but the benefits are tremendous in exposure and awareness of your site. Smaller, less expensive ways your organization can take part in state tourism programs include offering discount coupons on their websites or placing small listings in their published guides. Contact your state tourism commission and investigate the numerous methods by which your museum can be included in statewide promotion.

Other organizations make for perfect partners as well, like local chambers of commerce, downtown or Main Street organizations, and merchant associations. Local businesses thrive on the success of their neighboring cultural community, and you will often find that business organizations are more than happy to reprint your marketing information in their newsletters or on their websites, to post some of your printed material in their stores, or to cohost or sponsor special events benefiting your museum.

Your Own Best Critic: Analysis of Current Marketing Efforts

Unless your museum has just been established, you have probably invested some time, money, and effort into marketing up to this point. In creating a formal marketing plan, it is helpful to take a critical look at what has been done thus far and how it has succeeded (or not). In doing so, you can construct a method of evaluation that you can use to gauge the effectiveness of future marketing initiatives.

Revisit your last six months of marketing communication with an eye for trends. Were most of your marketing missives of only one type (i.e., press releases, news tips, newsletters, blog entries)? In order to launch a complete marketing program and connect with many different audiences, it is necessary to communicate on more than one front. Did you publicize only your upcoming events calendar, or did you make an effort to uncover discoveries and interesting news in all your museum's areas (e.g., collections, education, fundraising, buildings, and grounds)? In a marketplace hungry for information, there is a constant demand for new and interesting stories on many subjects, not just a list of an organization's coming attractions. Take note of areas in which your marketing has stagnated and make an effort to broaden your reach.

Experiment with drawing direct parallels between your marketing initiatives and the outcomes they produced. Did your press release result in a newspaper article written about your museum? Did that article drive more visitors to an upcoming event or spark more inquiries about an educational program? Can you see and measure the effects of your marketing efforts in media exposure, expanded visitation, or more donors? Write down all your current marketing moves for one month and record what specific effects they had on your museum. This will produce an easily discernable chart illustrating which initiatives are working and which are not.

Training yourself to recognize the eventual outcomes of your marketing efforts will work to your advantage when it comes to reporting to your board.

"If you don't know where you are going, you will wind up somewhere else."

—Yogi Berra

Outcome-based evaluation (OBE) is an invaluable tool for staffers who want to gauge not only their marketing output but also what finally results from it.

Rather than addressing the evaluation process after the marketing initiatives have been executed, include evaluation in the earliest parts of your marketing plan. This is key to OBE. Give careful thought not only to what steps to take in promoting a program or event but to what you want your marketing to accomplish ultimately. Take your goals to their logical ends. Do you simply want to raise awareness of your institution (a goal that is difficult to quantify and measure), or do you want to drive more visitors to your museum? Do you want visitors to convert to members or donors, and if so, what percentage of converted visitors would you like to aim for? Is your ambition to have your museum featured in x national publications this year, or is it to use that broadened exposure to increase site rental revenue? Be as specific as possible in outlining your goals to maximize measurability. Value-oriented goals (i.e., changing an audience's perceptions or behaviors) are important but almost impossible to measure; therefore, it is hard to gauge accomplishment. It is far easier to convince a board of marketing success with concrete numbers and percentages ("This year's event drew seventy-six more attendees than last year's") than it is to use generalities ("More people see us as important").

Once you have identified your specific goals, you can outline the steps required to realize them, which make up the substance of your strategic event and program promotion plan. Designing a logic model is the easiest and most coherent way to graph out the required steps between your final outcomes and the steps needed to achieve them. A logic model (see table 1.1) will clearly map out your marketing process and illustrate to your board how your inputs (activities) logically—and successfully—relate to your outcomes and goals.

There are limitations to the outcome-based approach. Measuring results can identify changes in behavior, but OBE cannot discern if measurable changes are happening solely as a result of marketing efforts or there are other factors to account for. Your museum may see an upswing in field trips after some printed publicity, for example, but much of that outcome may also be due to your educational efforts in reaching out to local teachers. Savvy marketing will not take the place of quality content, so you can be sure that marketing will never be the sole

Table 1.1. Outcome-Based Planning and Evaluation

Promotion for Civil War Exhibit Opening

Inputs (resources needed for project)	Activities (steps taken to produce outcomes)	Outputs (produced by activities)	Outcomes (changes in your audience as a result of your outputs)	Goals (long-term impact)
Staff time for promotion: six hours Staff time for expert interviews: two hours Staff time for coverage during exhibit opening: five hours Budget: $200 for newspaper display advertising	One month in advance: Purchase display advertising (budget: $200) in local newspapers Send press release to all newspapers and broadcast stations within the target market Upload community calendar information online to newspapers and broadcast stations Update "Events Calendar" on museum website, social media sites Reprint press release on blog—include photos from exhibit construction Send press alert to newspaper editors regarding pre-opening exhibit sneak peek	Articles in both local newspapers; community calendar listings in media outlets throughout the target market Interview with curator and exhibit designer on local television station morning program RSVPs through social media sites will help staff to plan for attendees	At least two hundred visitors on opening day of exhibit Five to ten new museum members or donors Opening day visitors will view collection artifacts relating to the Civil War and share their impressions with others, driving repeat visits	Increased exposure to and appreciation for nineteenth-century military artifacts Expanded knowledge of museum services Expanded outreach into the community

cause of increased visitation, an increase in support, or a boosted endowment. But specific cause-and-effect data can go a long way in demonstrating to your board—and yourself—the importance of consistent marketing.

Building a Strategic Marketing Plan

There are a thousand ways to market a cultural institution, and undoubtedly a thousand things about your museum are inherently marketable. Combined, these may present an almost unconquerable mountain of possibilities, of tasks to undertake so that the right audiences hear the right things about each facet of your organization. It is easy to feel overwhelmed. Combat your apprehensions right away by using the intrinsic fun of marketing to dilute the tedium of planning. An enjoyable and illuminating method that I have used to kick-start the planning process is called memory mapping.

Memory mapping is not only for computer programmers. Each museum (zoo, theme park, public garden, etc.) boasts of those surefire spots that visitors remember most: places that inspire guests to comment to their companions, snap a photo, or linger a bit longer in appreciation of what they are seeing or learning. These are undoubtedly your strongest selling points, and they may not always be the spots you would think.

Start by sketching out a map of your museum. Skip the minute details, but be sure to include all the public spaces, inside and out. With your map, watch visitors as they tour your facility. Mark the places that visitors seemed to enjoy most (see figure 1.1). Note where people take photographs, especially where they take pictures of themselves or members of their party in front of specific things. These are the spots your guests feel are emblematic of their experience at your museum: the places and objects that they will associate with your museum when they remember their visit later. Take a good inventory of your memory map hot spots—the things that resonated with your current visitors are the most powerful things you can use to attract others to visit and support your museum.

At the General Lew Wallace Study & Museum, almost every visitor's camera is pointed at the exterior of General Wallace's extraordinary study building. Its striking rust-colored brick facade is attended by a forty-foot tower and ringed with a limestone frieze featuring hand-carved faces representing characters from Wallace's novels. The study is undeniably the centerpiece of our museum. So it follows that representations of the study building are foremost in all our marketing materials. Our logo is a stylized graphic of the study. Our brochures and rack cards feature a large, high-resolution photo of the study building against a clear blue sky. In almost all publications in which our listing appears, it is attended by a prominent photo of that iconic study. It is not an accident that we promote the building almost as much as we champion the man who built it. By utilizing the

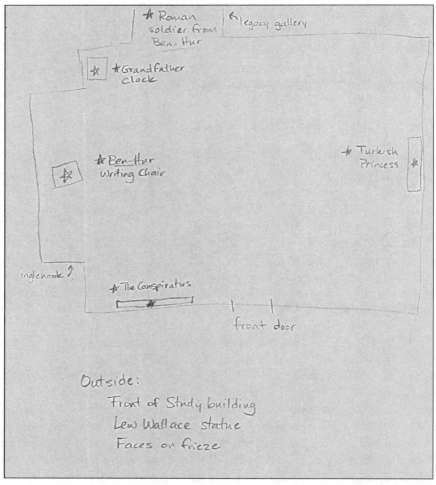

Figure 1.1. A memory map sketch of one of the rooms inside the General Lew Wallace Study & Museum, showing major areas or items that made the most impact with visitors.

strong visual appeal of the study, we can persuade others to come and be inspired by the building and its designer, as visitors before them have.

Keep your memory map in mind when formatting the rest of your marketing plan. Your most compelling images, artifacts, and stories will be the most persuasive and versatile weapons in your marketing arsenal, available to use in a multitude of different formats.

The first step in launching a marketing strategy for a fledgling organization is to establish a brand identity. A brand is your museum's public face. It encompasses the images, words, and feelings you want to elicit in people when they think of your institution.

An organization's brand extends from its name and mission statement to logos, letterhead, colors, typefaces, and tag lines. A museum brand can bring forth images of an institution's central figure or glimpses of a historical era. Your museum's brand will be utilized in all aspects of communication with your audience, so it is crucial to take the time to build something that lasts.

If you have not already, convene your board, staff, and key constituents for a series of brainstorming meetings to solidify your organization's formal name, logo, and typeface. (If you think issues as mundane as typefaces are not important, consider how hesitant you would be to drink a bottle of Coke labeled with something other than Coca-Cola's distinctive script.) Choose classic characteristics that resist trends and will not have to be changed as styles change. Choose a distinctive logo and typeface that will set your organization apart from your competitors, but do not make them so unusual as to be unreadable from a distance or difficult for commercial printers to reproduce. Try to get a consensus on these very important decisions from board members and staff, as

---

TEXTBOX 1.3

THINGS TO CONSIDER WHEN ESTABLISHING A BRAND IDENTITY

- Does the name of your organization succinctly convey everything that your museum is, while still being short enough to say in one breath?
- Is your name unique enough to differentiate your museum in a national or international market? There are hundreds of "Old Jail Museums" but only one Rotary Jail Museum in Crawfordsville, Indiana.
- Choose an easy-to-read typeface that will reproduce well in both large (highway signs and billboards) and small (lapel pins and business cards) format.
- Choose a color or small palette of colors that reflect the tone of your museum, and ensure that they work in a number of different formats (your logo may look lovely in rose pink, but try selling many T-shirts in that color to men).
- Can your logo be reprinted easily using a number of techniques like screen printing (for apparel) and vinyl cutting (on banners and signs)?
- Slogans and tag lines are not necessary to a successful brand and must be used sparingly and tastefully. Skip cute or funny and use a bare minimum of words to convey your strongest asset.

branding decisions reach almost every person in an organization and are difficult to change. These are the building blocks that you will use to construct the rest of your marketing strategy.

When you begin to work your brand identity into your marketing plan, be sure to remain consistent. Audiences will not get the chance to identify your museum through your brand if you make several content changes over a short period. Your name and logo should remain the same in every piece of communication you create, and even minor identity changes should be made only after thorough agreement has been reached that what you are currently using is not helping your institution reach its goals. It takes a very long time for an audience to adjust to an organization's change in public persona, and small alterations to your brand that seem inconsequential to you may cause just enough disruption for some people to lose confidence in what you have worked so hard to build.

Once you have forged your brand materials, it is time to put them to good use.

Budget Considerations

As is the case in most small museums, you will probably find that marketing funds are hard to come by. A small museum is dedicated to many important goals, and marketing considerations may pale when artifact stabilization or operating funds are at stake. Keeping this in mind, getting the most impact out of your marketing budget is one goal of constructing a thorough plan.

Work with your board and director to secure a firm amount for your marketing budget; then, using your logic models, identify the areas where money needs to be spent throughout your operating year. In most cases, the biggest percentage of marketing dollars will go to advertising and printing. Determine times in your calendar when purchasing advertising will garner the most response, usually before museum events, educational programs, or membership drives. Contact your local newspapers, television and radio stations, and the editors of your preferred travel publications for cost estimates, and sketch out a rough calendar of what advertisements you would like to buy, in which media, on what dates. This will help you plot out your available funds throughout the course of a year rather than overspending on the first few events you need to promote and leaving little for later. Follow the same approach with printing: Determine the times in your calendar year when printed materials (like brochures, rack cards, and event calendars) will make the most impact, gather job estimates, and plan your budget with a thought to purchasing possible replenishment runs when your initial stock runs low.

When you have plotted out your spending calendar for the year, do not worry if it looks sparse. Some of the most effective tools for marketing, public relations, and communication do not cost a thing, as this chapter explores in depth later. We cover paid methods of marketing initially, as you will want to plot out your marketing calendar in line with your budget first; after that, you will fill in the thin areas of your calendar with tricks and tactics that will more than supplement the money you will be spending. Let us begin our analysis of marketing strategy with advertising, a form of promotion that costs money, surely, but does not have to be prohibitively expensive when you know how to make the most of what you spend.

Advertising

The American public is bombarded with advertising every day in almost every aspect of life. From the moment our alarm clocks crash through our slumber with the local car lot's best deals to the end of the day when we drift back to sleep watching celebrities promote their latest movies on late-night television, our consciousness is infused with product pitches. Advertising revenues hit $285.1 billion in the United States in 2008,[4] reaching audiences through newspapers and magazines, television and radio, billboards, the Internet, mobile devices, movie screens, and the sides of buses, to name just a few methods. Advertising is very, very big business, and it may seem almost completely out of reach to small, nonprofit cultural organizations.

To add to the bad news, trends indicate that traditional advertising is getting less and less effective over time. With the advent of digital video recorders and satellite radio, audiences can fast-forward through those expensive advertisements or avoid them entirely. Spam filters and pop-up blockers on the Internet bat pesky ads away like flies. For all the money being spent in the advertising industry, less impact is being felt by the target audience. Money is going to waste, and for small museums, wasting money is a blasphemous practice.

Taking advantage of advertising does not have to break your marketing budget. There are several ways to boost the effectiveness of ads while keeping prices in a reasonable range.

First, remember to utilize your partners. Several organizations, like your local CVB or historical society, may be able to supply grant funds for promotion. Your CVB likely does its own advertising, regionally and statewide, in which your organization can be included for little or no cost. Talk to your regional sales executive for your state's tourism bureau to learn about inexpensive ways to include your museum in the bureau's promotional pieces. Since state tourism bureaus send their promotional pieces throughout the country as well as internationally to potentially interested travelers, you have a great opportunity for very wide exposure to an engaged, interested audience for a modest to moderate investment.

Look also to your partners for cooperative advertising at the state, regional, and local levels. Partnering with other area museums, for example, to purchase a

15

display advertisement in a newspaper in a nearby large city can dramatically cut costs while producing an attractive, persuasive ad that will be seen by a diverse audience.

Co-op advertising can also make expensive media like television and outdoor advertising more affordable to cultural organizations. Partnering with a few other museums on a thirty-second television ad could carry significant impact, depending on the station and the time of day. When considering television advertising, it is best to work with local or regional stations whose audiences are in your target market. These stations are less expensive than the ones in large metropolitan areas, and although their reach is smaller, you may find that response to your ads in relation to dollars spent is better even than for the "big guys."

Purchasing ad space with a few partners sweetens the deal even further, raising the interesting content of the ad while slashing the cost. Still, television advertising frequently carries an enormous cost, and although TV stations promise huge audiences, unless your ad carries a specific call to action (like dialing a phone number or visiting a website), it is difficult to gauge the true impact of your television campaign. Traditional television advertising is only recommended if you have a large marketing budget and a very compelling offer that urges a specific viewer response. We cover more effective and budget-friendly methods for working with television later in this chapter.

Outdoor advertising, which can also be an expensive enterprise with significant audience reach, can be purchased cooperatively, but it is advisable to only include one other partner. Outdoor advertising, depending on location, is most effective with very few words and large, strong images to catch the attention of automobile traffic. Cluttering the space with more than two advertisers will dilute your images and possibly make your text too small for travelers to read as they speed by.

With outdoor advertising, it makes more sense to purchase billboards in more populated areas within your target market, inside city limits rather than on interstate highways. Highways promise an endless stream of viewers, but only a fraction of them will be staying in the area long enough to consider visiting your museum or coming to your event. Inside the city, commuters are more likely to live or work in the area, increasing the chance that they will be interested in your site. Inside an urban area, the traffic is usually slower, allowing travelers a longer interval to look at your ad.

To maximize your outdoor advertising coverage inside a city, opt for an advertisement that is moved to different billboards in the area every month or few months. You can get more thorough city coverage with a single-billboard price, and your message remains fresh, as people pay more attention to new billboard images than to those that have been in one place for several months.

Radio advertising is another media outlet with significant reach. Radio stations charge a set amount per ad spot, depending on the length of the spot and the time of day it airs. As is the case with television, radio ads can be very expensive on larger stations with wide audiences, and it is up to you to decide if the exposure you receive is worth the money you spend. Both radio and TV stations can give you audience statistics for specific times of day, which will help you decide which hours carry the biggest chance of reaching your target market (of course, no audience statistics can accurately gauge how many viewers or listeners are actually paying attention to advertisements). In radio, the largest audiences tune in during morning and afternoon drive times, and a station's ad rates will reflect that. If a radio station can boast a particularly popular deejay or show host, the audience numbers (and ad prices) will go up even further.

What does that mean for a marketer? With a few exceptions, radio stations enjoy a more captive audience, as opposed to remote-wielding TV fans. Radio listeners are in their cars, with fewer distractions, and they are more likely to stay tuned to their chosen stations through commercial breaks. Some businesses, like restaurants and retail stores, will play a radio station throughout the day, giving advertisers exposure to an always-changing group of customers.

But radio is hardly a surefire method for reaching listeners. With personal listening devices like MP3 players and satellite radio being made compatible with car stereos, travelers can program their own musical drive accompaniment with no outside interruption. Many businesses utilize satellite radio or purchase a custom music service like Muzak expressly for the purpose of blocking out advertisements. And radio lacks the visual component that makes so many television advertisements memorable.

If you would like to invest in radio advertising, consider choosing local stations or smaller regional stations within your target market. Rates will be more affordable, and your audience will more likely be close enough to your location to be interested in a visit, event, or program. Do invest in spots that air during drive times, as audiences are significantly larger then than during any other segment of the day. If you have a very limited budget but still want to try radio, inquire into sponsorships, where your museum can sponsor a segment ("This weather break is sponsored by . . . ," for example) for a lower price than a full spot. Listeners are paying more attention during sponsored segments (weather, news, contests, or special broadcasts) than during a long block of similar-sounding advertisements. This tactic also works well in television; contact your local stations for details.

Read All about It: Newspaper Advertising

Newspaper advertising has long been the dependable choice for marketers who want to spread the word about their museums to a loyal local audience.

Even though newspapers are said to be a dying breed, rapidly losing ground to websites where users can find on-demand information, you probably still cannot think of too many households that do not subscribe to at least one newspaper. Especially in smaller cities, newspapers still dedicate themselves to local news to a degree not extensively seen on the Internet. Utilizing newspapers makes sense as well when you consider your museum's target audience. Most cultural organizations seek to attract adults aged thirty to sixty-five, one of newspapers' largest consumer bases.

Placing a display ad—a large advertisement with images and text—is usually the best bet for newspaper advertising with the most impact. Depending on a newspaper's readership and the size of an ad, rates for display ads can run from $50 to hundreds, even thousands, of dollars. Placement is key when purchasing display ads; many newspapers place advertisements in groups along the bottom or edges of pages, with more ads in the center sections than in the first or last few pages. Grouping ads together is the most efficient way for newspapers to lay out their pages, but you risk losing readers if your ad is buried in a sea of similar-looking displays. Newspaper advertising representatives may offer preferred placement for a slightly higher rate, which involves running ads in sections that usually experience greater readership, like the sports or local news pages. The success rate with this approach is spotty, however, and it is up to you to decide whether the extra charge is worth it.

Many newspapers now run advertisements on the sacred space of their front pages, which used to be reserved for only the most pressing news articles of the day. Although it is a more common practice to sell ads only on the bottom half of the front page ("below the fold"), some papers are selling coveted real estate above the fold, most likely as a response to the industry's recent loss in revenue. One approach used by newspapers today is to sell the "ear," or top-right corner of the front page, as a spot for the advertiser's logo and a prompt for the reader to refer to a larger ad on an inside page. Other newspapers run a row of small, full-color display ads along the bottom or sides of the front page. Ad spaces above the fold are coveted by advertisers because of their prominence—they appear to everyone who even passes by a newspaper box or newsstand. Front-page ads are usually sold as multiple-ad packages, so you might face a bit of a commitment.

For noticeable display advertising inside the paper, focus your efforts on design and appeal. The newspaper you choose to work with will undoubtedly have advertising designers on staff; ask for examples of their work. Often you can get attractive, high-quality ad design with little or no increase in price. If you are not satisfied with the newspaper's design work, you can opt to try your own design or, if design is not your forte, to find an outside designer. Of course, hiring a gifted professional to design your ads entails an extra cost, but having a compelling design that stands out from the myriad of other ads in the paper can be worth it, depending on how long your ad runs and the size of the newspaper's readership.

Take a look at the newspaper in which you are preparing to advertise, especially the other ads. What are the various ad sizes; what is the most popular size? Are the ads largely text based, or do they include vivid images? What is the ratio of full-color to black-and-white ads? Do the ads include an irresistible call to action, or are they largely informational? In order to make your advertisement stand out, make your ad do whatever the neighboring ads do not. Include just a few words and a striking image of your site, for example, to make your ad eye-catching amid a sea of text. While many other ads use simple line art or clip art, a high-resolution photo (even in black and white) can look distinctive and compelling. Running a coupon, discount, or special within your ad will draw attention from ads that are largely declarative. Remember to stay true to your institution's mission and climate; often simply conveying your museum's sophistication is enough to make your ad stand out from the used car lots and grocery stores.

Another option in newspaper advertising is the freestanding insert ad or circular. Commonly used by retail stores, these separate, usually color sections of the newspaper are ads unto themselves, often including coupons. Since they literally stand on their own apart from regular newspaper content, insert ads are hard to ignore, and that makes them tremendously valuable to advertisers. Although production costs for inserts may run high, especially for extras like glossy paper or perforated coupons, you can keep insert ads within your

---

TEXTBOX 1.4

QUESTIONS TO ASK WHEN PURCHASING ADVERTISING IN ANY MEDIUM

- Will you provide current viewer/reader/listener/exposure demographic numbers so that I can gauge who is receiving my advertising message?
- Do you offer discounts or free extras (i.e., color printing, free listing in service directory) for nonprofit organizations?
- Can I get better advertising rates if I commit to a long-term purchase (six to twelve months on a billboard, for example)?
- Are there better days of the week to run advertising, or are there any special sections or programs in which I can advertise that would appeal to my target audience (bridal specials, summer-travel sections, etc.)?

budget by closely targeting your audience or choosing which newspapers will carry your inserts.

Like direct mail, newspapers can be segmented into zip codes that allow advertisers to choose which delivery zones their insert ads are delivered to. This works especially well in large urban markets where your museum is much closer to some neighborhoods than others, or if you are interested in targeting specific socioeconomic groups. Your insert ad appears only in your specific target markets, your costs stay much lower than for direct mail, and your ad is enveloped in a trusted news vehicle that people bring into their homes much more readily than perceived junk mail.

In smaller markets, although zip code segmentation may not be available, costs for insert ads can be much more affordable, and production costs can be as little as the cost of making an attractive full-page color copy. Insert ads stand out, and the price may not be as prohibitive as you might first believe. Talk to your local newspaper about your advertising options, and you will find there is an effective way to reach thousands of readers for almost every marketing budget.

In fact, there are limitless advertising options out there for marketers with a modest budget and a mind open to possibility. From ads on restaurant coasters to promotional lines in church bulletins, from yard signs to colorful displays on the backs of park benches to huge commercials that run on movie screens, you can communicate with your target audience in innumerable interesting and eye-catching ways. Be fearless and inquisitive in exploring the advertising options in your community, in your state, and across the country, and you may find yourself making your budget work far more effectively than you ever anticipated.

Public Relations: Taking It to the People

Do not despair when your budget gets tight and you have allocated most of your shoestring marketing budget on advertising your museum's programs and events. As many methods as there are involving advertising, there are tenfold more opportunities to share your organization's message in the world of public relations, and most of them cost nothing but your time.

Additionally, as inexpensive as public relations initiatives are, they can be even more attention grabbing than the brightest billboard or flashiest television ad. Think about what content in a newspaper catches your interest first: the display ads or the front-page news? Do television commercials attract a greater audience than the programs? Do you pay $12 a ticket at the movie theater to watch the previews or the motion picture? The facts are simple: In this age of information on demand, more and more people are tuning out advertising in favor of pure, interesting content. As a museum representative, you are in the enviable position of sharing some of the most fascinating, primary-source information with this increasingly news-hungry public, and public relations will be your most effective instrument for taking your message to the people.

The most basic and frequently used public relations tool is the press release. As a cultural institution, your museum has an endless supply of stories to share with its audience, including upcoming events, educational programs, artifact discoveries, outreach initiatives, research findings, membership drives, and grant awards. Sharing information of all kinds helps to keep your museum in the public eye, and as we have seen before, public awareness drives visitation, membership, endowment, and much more.

A press release is a news announcement submitted directly to media outlets, such as newspapers, television and radio stations, and even magazines or websites, depending on the nature of the information being released. A press release is designed to pique the interest of journalists in the hope that they will develop your information into a news story. Considering that they are quite effective and free of cost, press releases are one of the most commonly used public relations methods. Journalists, especially those in more populated markets, receive several, sometimes hundreds, of press releases each week, and your release needs to stand out among the flood for your intended media outlet to take interest.

In making your press release as attractive to news outlets as possible, pay close attention to construction and readability. Place the information especially pertinent to journalists at the top of the release, including the full name of your institution as you would like to have it printed, your contact name and phone number or e-mail address, the date your information can be released (in most cases, your release will specify "for immediate release"; if your information needs to be held back until a certain date or time, it is recommended that you save the entire release until you can announce it publicly), and whether you are including any supplemental material like logos or photos (see figure 1.2).

As you write your press release, remember to think more like a journalist and less like a marketer. Make it your mission to deliver the most compelling facts, not to sell something. News reporters put their "lead," or biggest piece of information, in the first paragraph of their stories to set the tone of the article and draw in audiences right away. Similarly, the main thrust of your release should be disclosed in the first paragraph. Editors who cannot discern the reason for your press release in the first couple of paragraphs may lose interest before they even get to its point.

Journalists support their facts with supplemental interviews, inserting quotes from authorities to bolster the integrity of the story. At your museum, the experts who can give credibility to your press release are often under the same roof; be sure to utilize their expertise at every opportunity. A press release about your museum's newest exhibit carries much more weight when peppered with quotes from your curator, education director, or exhibit fabricator. Quotes also make a release more readable and interesting to your audience than a list of informational points with no personal point of view.

Design the content of your press release just as a journalist would write an article, including proper grammar and punctuation, the correct names and titles of the people you have quoted, and the full information needed for the reader to understand the entire story. Make sure you have answered the mandatory journalistic questions: who, what, where, when, why, and who benefits. The more work you do to make your press release a readable article that needs little revision, the more likely your chosen media source will print or air exactly what

Press Release

Contact: Kara Edie, Marketing Coordinator
Phone: 765-362-5769
Email: kedie@ben-hur.com
Additional resources: related photos are available. Contact above for access.

For Immediate Release

HOLIDAY OPEN HOUSE IS MUSEUM'S LAST DAY OF SEASON

December 12 also the final day for public to view "Sanctuary" exhibit

CRAWFORDSVILLE, IN, December 2, 2010— The General Lew Wallace Study and Museum is hosting a free Holiday Open House and Volunteer Reception on their last operating day of 2010, Sunday, December 12 from 1:00 to 4:00 p.m.

The Open House takes place inside the Carriage House Interpretive Center, which is beautifully outfitted in yuletide décor, including a Christmas tree decorated in Victorian fashion. Festive activities and toasty treats will be on hand, as well as a fun holiday craft project for the kids.

The Museum will also be welcoming back its volunteers for a holiday party during the Open House. "We couldn't achieve a fraction of what we do without the work of our wonderful volunteers," said Kara Edie, Visitor Services & Marketing Director at the General Lew Wallace Study and Museum. "We're inviting all of our volunteers to the Open House as a relaxing get-together before the bustle of the holidays."

The Open House will also be the final opportunity for visitors to see the Museum's 2010 exhibit, *Sanctuary: Preserving the Legacy of Lew Wallace,* which includes some of General Wallace's personal artifacts that were removed from his Study just before the renovation on the 112-year-old building began earlier this year. The Museum will be closed through January and reopen for tours on Wednesday, February 2, 2011.

Admission to the Museum during the Holiday Open House is free. Call 765-362-5769 or email study@ben-hur.com for further information.

About GLWSM
"The General Lew Wallace Study and Museum celebrates and renews belief in the power of the individual spirit to affect American history and culture." With these words as their mission, the General Lew Wallace Study and Museum welcomes visitors from across the nation and around the world. As the location where Lew Wallace wrote Ben-Hur and the home of the world's largest collection of General Wallace's personal memorabilia, the Museum is an ideal visitors' destination for the bibliophile and the history buff alike. The Museum is owned and operated by the City of Crawfordsville Park & Recreation Department and governed by the Lew Wallace Study Preservation Society board of trustees. For more information about General Wallace and his magnificent study, visit www.ben-hur.com.

Figure 1.2. Sample press release.

you have given them. In this way, you can begin to control your message, rather than allowing a journalist to bend the story in a way you had not intended.

Press releases are not only for newspapers. Radio and television stations are required to broadcast public service announcements (PSAs) from nonprofit organizations as a percentage of their programming. You can submit event announcements or new information about your museum in the form of a press release that broadcast stations can easily adapt into PSAs, which can earn you hundreds of dollars in free advertising.

If a reporter or editor takes an interest in your press release, he or she will likely call your museum to ask supplementary questions, schedule an interview with one of your experts on staff, or drop by to take photographs or video. You can also make your press releases more attractive by providing some of this supplementary material beforehand, which makes your information more interesting and the journalist's job easier (which increases the chance that your release will be run). As an attachment to your release, specify the names and phone numbers or e-mail addresses of experts who can be interviewed for that particular story and a good time for a journalist to call. Especially when you are e-mailing releases, attaching a relevant photograph or two can pique reporters' interest, and they can choose to use your photo in an article instead of taking their own. Make sure any photos you send to media outlets belong to your organization and that any identifiable people in your photos have given permission for their images to be published.

Members of the media are tremendously busy, and they cannot be expected to have as expert a knowledge of your museum as your staff does. Making reporters' work easier by crafting much of the article for them and providing the supplemental information they need will make them not only eager to run your current release but may inspire them to come back to your museum when they are working on a different story. Establishing your museum as a source of expertise among your local media outlets is a terrific way to build beneficial public relations in your community.

For news that necessitates a more dynamic approach than a standard release, consider utilizing media alerts or advisories. Media alerts invite members of the press, in groups or individually, to visit your site in advance of breaking news or events. Usually much briefer than press releases, alerts immediately answer the who, what, where, when, and why questions that journalists require with little extra information or quoted material. In an alert, you will specify the date, time, and duration of the period for which you will be making your experts available for interviews on a pertinent topic and establishing why this topic is important to the news outlet's readers, listeners, or viewers. Remember to include detailed directions for reaching your museum and a phone number or e-mail address to respond to if a reporter has questions or cannot attend.

Media advisories are especially useful in advance of your museum's events. Make a point of inviting your local media representatives to newsworthy events taking place at your museum, and be sure to give them notice well in advance so they can plan for their attendance. Let them know of the expert interviewees on your staff who will be present at the event and the specific times of speeches, presentations, awards, or other photo opportunities they may want to take advantage of. Sending photographs of previous or similar events can also be useful for media representatives to know what to expect. Being proactive in inviting local reporters, rather than simply promoting your event and hoping that reporters arrive, will increase the chances of your event's receiving media coverage and raise the profile of your museum.

And how do you get the public to your events with no cost? Almost every type of media outlet utilizes a community calendar in which it informs its audiences of upcoming programs in their neighborhood. Sending short, to-the-point calendar notices regarding your museum exhibits, programs, and events can be an effective, and free, method of promotion. Since media outlets need significant advance notice to include your event in their calendars, it is helpful to establish a marketing calendar that runs in conjunction with your events calendar throughout the year, reminding you to submit community calendar items and news tips to media outlets at least three to four weeks in advance of each event. You can make submissions to most newspapers' and radio and television stations' community calendars online using simple forms. These outlets promote upcoming cultural programs as a service to their communities, and it is likely that your events are just what they are interested in promoting. Investigate the policies of each of the preferred media outlets in your target market and consistently provide your content so that they can pass it on to their audiences.

A key to simple, productive public relations is to keep in mind that your museum is a terrific source of interesting information that news organizations—and their audiences—want to hear about. If done properly, communicating your news tips to websites, publications, and broadcast stations will help to make reporters' jobs easier. Do not keep your stories to yourself; share everything from a change in leadership to a new children's program to a fascinating detail you have just learned about an artifact. These stories are news, and establishing your museum as a consistent source of remarkable news will unfailingly attract news sources and the people who subscribe to them.

Online Marketing: Public Relations on a Global Scale

"It's a new world out there" is becoming sort of a cliché in describing the amazing changes being brought about by the introduction of the Internet, but for history organizations, the maxim could not be more apt. In our field, we are accustomed to being the strict stewards of our collections, putting interconnectivity and transparency to the public far behind issues of security and longevity.

But it is indeed a new world out there, and more and more people across the globe are utilizing the Internet for everything from banking to accessing daily news to finding a mate. The percentage of Americans who are online has reached nearly 80 percent, spanning all demographics and ages. According to the U.S. Travel Association, over 90 million Americans use the Internet for travel planning.[5] Tourism attractions of every stripe are accessible on the Internet, from theme parks to museums to zoos. Organizations not represented on the Internet risk falling behind their competitors with every passing month.

Although there are very effective methods of advertising on the Web (a couple of which we will touch on later), the Internet is foremost a public relations domain where museums can connect and communicate with their customers on a more personal, grassroots level. The Internet is fertile ground in which a cultural institution's advocates can gather, stay informed, and attract new followers, as well as support the organization financially.

Blogs

A basic and easy method by which a museum can dip its toes in the vast waters of the Internet is through a Web log, or blog. A blog is a type of website featuring a regularly updated series of posts with information, photos, videos, and links to other websites. More informal and conversational than a website, a blog gives your museum the versatility to post articles of any type any time, without going through the hassle of submitting them to traditional media outlets. Any number of people on your museum's staff can contribute to a single blog; in fact, having several different authors from throughout your museum can give your blog a multivoice feel that makes it more interesting to readers.

Blogs can be constructed and incorporated into your site in a number of different ways. If you or a member of your staff is proficient in hypertext markup language (HTML) or another website-creation language, you can create your blog from scratch with a word processing program, customize your blog to whatever specifications you choose, and integrate it seamlessly with your main website. Like most of us, however, if you have little or no coding experience, you still have a multitude of options.

There are paid blog services especially for companies and organizations that will take you step by step through the blogging process to create an attractive and easy-to-update blog with a unique domain name (e.g., yourblog.com) that is easy for visitors to remember. Paid services also connect your blog to their large communities, which helps your blog appear more prominently and more often in search engines like Yahoo! and Google. With a paid service, your blog will have a clean, ad-free look and extensive visitor tracking, which makes it easy to see who is visiting your blog, where visitors are from, and what is bringing them there. Paid services usually cost between $5 and $150 a month, depending on the number of visitors to your blog.

There are also plenty of high-quality, free blog hosts, two of the largest currently being Blogger.com and WordPress.com. Free blogs can be constructed and updated by users of every skill level; Blogger and WordPress both feature eye-catching design templates that can be customized and set up in minutes. With free services, your blog domain resides on your host's server, so your domain name will usually have a derivative of your host's name in it (like yourblog.blogspot.com or yourblog.wordpress.com). This makes your blog address somewhat harder for visitors to remember when trying to locate your blog. If you are trying a free blog service, choose a blog domain name that is short and easy to identify as belonging to your museum. For example, the blog name of the General Lew Wallace Study & Museum, a legendarily lengthy moniker, has been shortened to wallacestudy.blogspot.com.

Once you have set up your blog, it is important to update it consistently. Blog visitors are looking for new, interesting information and are less likely to return to your blog if they see no changes after a couple of visits. By recruiting authors from around your museum—from visitor services to collections to the gift shop—you can fashion content that is varied, fresh, and compelling to all your blog readers.

Since blogs are less formal and constricting than regular media, you can feel free to include blog posts that give more of a behind-the-scenes, day-by-day view of your museum, as well as articles that qualify as more important breaking news. Mention your upcoming events in your blog posts, as well as new research developments or artifact discoveries. Important news from your partner organizations or new information from the museum field may be interesting to your blog readers as well; include links in your posts to other articles, websites, or blogs to point your readers to additional facts. Sometimes, even a pleasing photograph of your building or grounds can pique your readers' enthusiasm.

Take advantage of the Internet's simple sharing interfaces by including in your blog entries methods by which readers can easily distribute your content via e-mail or to social media and bookmarking sites like Facebook, Digg, and Twitter. This enables your visitors to spread your content to vast audiences with just a click of the mouse. Almost every blog publisher will also automatically broadcast your blog posts as an RSS feed, a Web feed format that allows visitors to subscribe to regularly updated works through their own RSS readers and makes it easier for your visitors to return to view your content repeatedly over time.

Most blogs include a comment feature that allows your readers to share their opinions and submit feedback on articles that interest them; this gives your blog a social, conversational quality and enables your visitors to feel more connected to your organization. Sometimes blog visitors will spark fascinating conversation and debate within your blog's comment section, which enhances the visitor experience and keeps people coming back to your blog. Always enable comments on your blog posts; if you find you encounter problems with spam—or unrelated, promotional, or rude comments—you can apply a setting whereby you moderate comments before they are posted live to your blog.

When people discover that your blog is a varied, dynamic community where their voices are heard and responded to, they will return to view your content again and again, and you may pleasantly discover that your blog is one of the most productive gateways into your physical location, with blog visitors becoming museum visitors, supporters, and members.

Microblogging

Taking the casualness and immediacy of blogging to an even further extreme is microblogging, featured on the tremendously popular site Twitter.com. On Twitter, blog posts are limited to 140 characters, the maximum length of a text message on most mobile devices. Twitter posts, or "tweets," are posted to Twitter.com or any number of Twitter's compatible reader applications to be viewed by a person's or organization's readers, who "follow" them in order to keep up with the latest messages. Organizations commonly use Twitter to point readers to longer posts on their blogs or interesting articles on their websites, to share links to partner organizations or news from the museum field, or to post photos. Twitter photos are usually hosted separately on compatible sites like TwitPic.com, and links to those photos are embedded in tweets.

Again, whether your museum realizes a benefit from the microblogging trend depends on the energy invested in the medium and the level of consistency. Since Twitter is incredibly fast paced and people usually follow hundreds or thousands of people who each post several times a day, an organization would need to post interesting factual tidbits, compelling photos, or links to other articles or sites at least once a day just to keep up. Fortunately, Twitter publishing platforms like TweetDeck can run unobtrusively in the background of your computer desktop and can be easily accessed when your museum has interesting items to share.

The real strength of Twitter lies not in its publishing but in its access to a much wider conversation. Millions of people use Twitter every day to comment on everything from the mundane (what they had for breakfast, for example) to important news items that affect the international community. Twitter was one of the major methods by which people voiced their outrage over the Gulf of Mexico oil disaster in 2010. Discussion and debate are happening on Twitter in real time, and, more than likely, issues that touch or directly affect your organization are currently being discussed. TweetDeck, Tweetie, or other Twitter clients can alert you when words or phrases connected to your museum are being tweeted so that you can monitor the conversation and connect to those who are talking about your institution. This helps you easily communicate with like-minded parties and potential museum supporters without spending hours searching for them. And participating in a conversation with those people interested in your organization can easily convert fans into supporters, donors, and members.

Social Media

One of the biggest Internet trends of the last decade has been the boom in social media. The rather nebulous and fluid term *social media* includes the various online tools and technologies that allow people to create content, communicate, and share information with one another. No longer is news solely the domain of media gatekeepers who decide when and where information is disseminated to the public. News articles can now be generated, published, dispersed, altered, and critiqued on the Internet by users themselves—for free.

Social media websites are tremendously popular, but their shelf lives are limited and their popularity is fleeting. Specific websites mentioned in this chapter may no longer be relevant when this book is published. But no matter the channel, the precept is the same: People want to interact with companies, including museums and cultural organizations, on a more personal level, and Internet technology now makes it easy to do so. Those organizations who do not take advantage of the opportunity to meet with their audiences in this new medium put themselves at a disadvantage.

Facebook.com is the trend leader in social media at the moment, enjoying a membership of over 300 million users across the globe. Facebook is a utility by which people can connect to friends, family, coworkers, and classmates to share everything from photos and videos to blog posts and applications. Facebook is valuable to marketers not only for the ability to communicate with target audiences but also for innovations like company pages, which are platforms set up by Facebook for businesses and organizations to establish a social media presence for themselves that visitors can view whether they are Facebook members or not.

Facebook pages allow organizations to keep in touch with their constituents in a more approachable environment, where an institution that may be regarded as academic and stuffy can communicate with fans in a friendlier manner. Your museum can post its location, hours of operation, parking, and

Figure 1.3. The Facebook fan page for the General Lew Wallace Study & Museum.

public transportation options on the page's "Info" tab for prospective visitors, and for those who live farther away, you can include photos and video of your museum's events and programs. Pages include an "Events" category where your museum can post upcoming events complete with details, photos, times, and maps to each event's location.

Facebook works easily with numerous other Internet platforms so you can integrate your museum's other social media initiatives into your Facebook page. If your museum utilizes YouTube for hosting videos, for example, you can include a YouTube section within your Facebook page where visitors can view all your YouTube videos without leaving the Facebook site. With a robust fan page, you will find the ease of accessibility Facebook provides boosts the popularity of all the programming you do across the Internet.

Nonprofit organizations can also benefit from Facebook's global reach through its Causes application, a tool by which Facebook users can promote their preferred charities among their networks of friends. Organizations can raise funds or promote special needs through the Causes application while keeping funders updated on the progress of projects through photos, blog posts, links, and videos. Your museum can link its Causes page to its fan page, making it easy for followers to access and contribute content.

Facebook is a free service supported by advertising. As a Facebook user, you will most likely notice small graphic and text ads on the right-hand side of most pages. For users, this represents only a small inconvenience for the privilege of accessing Facebook's many features without charge. In fact, Facebook uses detailed audience targeting and feedback mechanisms to broadcast ads that ensure most users will only see advertising that appeals to their interests or is relevant to their geographical area, so many Facebook ads are seen as supplemental to the online experience instead of as an unwanted nuisance. Users who frequent the fan pages of art museums in New England, for example, may view ads for other area art galleries or institutions of which they might have been unaware.

Taking advantage of Facebook's wide reach and pinpoint targeting with paid advertising is doable for every marketing budget, no matter how small. When you purchase advertising with Facebook, you will design a small text ad with one small photo (or your logo, whichever draws more attention and is more recognizable as your brand). You can choose to be billed for every time your ad is viewed (pay per impression) or every time a user clicks your ad and accesses your Facebook page or website (pay per click). Facebook allows you to bid for a specific price per click or impression and will run your ads more often for a higher bid price. You can set a daily spending limit of as little as $2 for your ad to guarantee that massive audiences will not run away with your advertising budget.

When targeting your ad, you can choose Facebook users in a specific location (within a predetermined number of miles from your site, for example, or within one of your target markets) or who have established an interest in one of your specialties (museums, European history, literature, Native Americans). This ensures that your ads will be shown to the audiences with the greatest chance of being interested in your content, and you will not waste valuable advertising dollars, for example, trying to promote your antique doll museum to twenty-five-year-old, male heavy-metal fans.

Advertising in other online venues can be productive, but before investing time and money in an online venture, make sure the website or Web application is used and trusted by a great number of users, that you can establish a spending cap in every ad campaign, and that your ad can be targeted to receptive audiences.

As with everything that happens online, the popularity of social networking sites like Facebook can be fleeting, and it is hard to determine the shelf life of an Internet endeavor so that you can make good decisions on where to invest your valuable time. Core audiences that frequent certain online communities are also susceptible to shifting, as was the case for Facebook when its most fervent users changed from almost exclusively college students in the early years of the medium to adults and seniors once they embraced benefits like networking and reconnecting with old friends.[6] Be cognizant that not every "next big thing" in the Internet world is going to be worth pouring your attention into, and not every Web trend, no matter how compelling, is going to result in a return on investment for your museum. Stay connected to other museums in your discipline to distinguish Internet tools that effectively work for museums from fleeting online fads that can ultimately be a waste of effort. Spend time at regional and national conferences to discover the newest Internet initiatives that are working for other museums, and ask questions about how you can tailor them to your purposes. Delve into the online presences of other museums in your field and in your area to see what Web tools they are using successfully, and do not be afraid to co-opt a good idea for your own museum. You do not need to reinvent the wheel; you just need to make the wheel fit your vehicle and use it to take your museum to new places.

Tending the Seed: Nurturing Relationships Online and Off

The most effective and rewarding facets of marketing involve the establishment and nourishment of relationships, online and in "real life." Once you have attracted an audience through advertising and public relations, it is imperative to give these people a reason to stay committed to your museum. This involves listening and responding appropriately to your visitors' concerns, keeping them interested and involved, and letting them know of their inestimable value to your organization.

The relative effortlessness of communication between organizations and their fans on social media sites like Facebook can facilitate the growth of affinity groups and customer evangelists. Your institution's most fervent supporters can use your Facebook fan page to voice their opinions on topics important to them and to give feedback about your museum's programs and policies, which can foster tremendously positive public relations effects when handled correctly.

When your fans begin to communicate with your institution through Facebook, for example, or your blog or other online site, foster the growing relationship by responding politely, helpfully, and enthusiastically. Provide your commenters with further information on a topic, supplemental links, or additional reading. Refer their queries to the appropriate experts in your museum or in your field, and treat online visitors with the same care and attention you would give to a guest to your physical location. Never be rude or dismissive, as negative reactions to your online initiatives will reflect poorly on your museum and can spread with shocking speed to millions of users across the Internet. Providing a positive experience for your online visitors will likely inspire them to share your site with their friends, and you will have harnessed the Internet's massive power of communication for the ultimate benefit of your museum.

Newsletters

In the realm of nurturing relationships, you will find that your public relations job does not end once you have hooked the members of your target audience and brought them into your museum. One of your most effective methods of communication with members and supporters is a newsletter, and recipients can enjoy receiving valuable information from your regular news communiqués whether through the mail or via the Internet.

31

DOS AND DON'TS OF NURTURING ONLINE DISCUSSION

- Do identify yourself when representing your museum on the Internet. People are more likely to communicate with a real person than a disembodied voice speaking for the museum.
- Do take part in the conversation that grows on your website, blog, and social media sites, but do not feel that you have to respond to every comment made.
- Do express your appreciation for compliments and positive comments, even if you simply extend a general thank-you to a large group of people.
- Do not be offended or rattled by negative comments. Do try to identify the problem that incited the comment and work to provide a solution.
- Do not ever respond to negative comments with anger or insults. Public relations catastrophes have mushroomed on the Internet because a company representative did not take the time to think before responding. Always view the situation from the customer service prospective, and try to turn negative experiences into positive ones.
- Do not plant positive comments in your online communities or pretend not to be affiliated with your organization. This practice, called "Astroturfing" because it fakes a grassroots public response, will undermine your credibility and drive genuine commenters away.

Newsletters have been cultural organizations' most reliable messengers for a long time, and with good reason. As periodic missives to your target audiences and proven supporters, newsletters contain articles of interest to funders, constituents, fans, and partner organizations alike. By publishing a consistent newsletter, you can keep your community updated on your most pressing news, attract new visitors, and convert visitors into members or supporters.

The length and content of newsletters varies depending on the organization, the frequency of publication, and the amount of information to transmit. You can produce your newsletters in-house with a computer and copier, or you may choose to have your newsletter printed professionally, contingent on your budget and technological requirements.

Format your newsletters as newspapers do, with equal portions of breaking news and interesting features, firsthand accounts from throughout your organization, and attractive photos. Enlist the writing talents of several members of your staff or volunteers to give your newsletter a multifaceted voice.

Since your newsletter will likely be received by potential visitors as well as members and established supporters, make sure each issue includes basic information relating to your museum, such as your address, admission fees, and hours of operation. Listing information such as your website and blog addresses is also important for readers who want to delve further into your site. If one purpose of your newsletter is to solicit funds, be sure to incorporate a method by which potential donors can contribute (such as a phone number or a website), or include a reply device that donors can return to your museum.

Although you may use it to solicit funds and attract potential visitors, do not treat your newsletter solely as a marketing device. A newsletter is the place for your museum to shine—to showcase what your organization has accomplished and educate the public about its mission and mandate. Write compelling and informative articles that include the who, what, where, when, and why components of journalists' news stories. Add credibility to your claims with primary sources and direct quotes from the experts in your organization. Inserting graphs, charts, or other illustrative graphics can enhance the coherence of more technical articles.

Naturally, your newsletter is the perfect place to promote your upcoming events, exhibits, and programs, which can serve as an invitation for your members and visitors to join you. During an event, take photographs and act as a journalist would, noting the ambience of the occasion and the activities that took place to include in the newsletter for members who could not attend.

You should also use your newsletter to recognize and publicly thank the members, supporters, volunteers, and staff who keep your museum running. A regular feature of your newsletters should be a page listing the people and businesses who have contributed to your organization since the publication of your last issue. Remember also to list any anonymous donations: Even donors who prefer to remain unnamed will be pleased to see your appreciation.

Additionally, it is a best practice to use your newsletter to recognize grants and awards received from public funding sources. In fact, many funders require that their grant awards be publicized in your regular publications. Include grants and gifts of any size and for any purpose; you may wish to include grants that span a long-term duration in more than one newsletter during the grant period.

Invite topical experts to write articles on a regular basis. This helps spread the mission of your organization by informing readers about your central figure, genre, or history. The fascinating articles that your researchers and archivists can produce will remind your visitors of the central significance of your museum and keep them invested in your continuing projects.

Other staff members, volunteers, or board members within your organization can also be valuable contributors to your newsletter. Ask your grounds manager to write a regular column on the seasonal demands and fruits of your museum gardens, for example. For readers fascinated by behind-the-scenes artifact discoveries, include a regular contribution from your curatorial staff, complete with photos of objects that cannot currently be seen on display. Interesting revelations from throughout your museum that readers look forward to will make your newsletter a valuable "perk" that you can utilize as a special incentive for members, partners, and donors.

Depending on the size of your newsletter and the number of different authors contributing to it, you will want to begin soliciting articles and photos for the next issue more than a month in advance of publication. Use a quality desktop publishing program such as Adobe InDesign or Microsoft Publisher to lay out newsletter pages in a clean and attractive format. Pore over each article to minimize errors in spelling and punctuation, and have two or three other people proofread it to ensure accuracy. Make sure the details of each newsletter issue remain the same over time. Changes in font size and face, photo borders, and caption style can look unprofessional and be jarring to readers if they happen with every issue. Design a banner for the front page of your newsletter that is emblematic of your museum; take care to keep your banner consistent so readers will recognize your newsletter when it arrives in their mailboxes.

If you plan to mail the newsletter to your audience through the postal service, remember to include white space to affix address labels, your return address, and postage. If delivering it electronically, you may choose to save your digital newsletter pages as portable document format (PDF) files or as images that can be viewed on any type of computer. PDF files can also be uploaded to your website and shared through e-mail or social media networks.

If your desktop publishing skills are lacking, several e-mail marketing firms can put your museum's information into an attractive template sent to recipients as an e-mail newsletter. Though these services cost money, it may be well worth the investment to utilize a company that can streamline your information into a readable format and deliver it reliably to your contact list. Paid e-mail services will also help you to manage your contacts by adding new recipients who sign up through your website and removing people who e-mail a wish to unsubscribe. Look up e-mail marketing on the Internet for reviews of trusted providers, and talk to your partner organizations about services that work well for them.

Remember that no matter the format, your newsletter is a published record of the activities, goals, and accomplishments of your organization, so ensure that your content is always in line with the standards your museum has established and the best practices of your industry. Once published and distributed, the information you submit becomes public record and cannot be changed; aim for the highest quality at all times.

Nurturing relationships with visitors and supporters is not only the job of the museum marketer; it should be a priority for everyone involved with the organization. Your museum director can be instrumental in communicating to new donors how much their investment and attention means. Members of your board of trustees can be your most eloquent defenders, spreading that valuable word-of-mouth message to members of the community from their unique behind-the-scenes perspective. Those passionate supporters within and around your museum can be the most effective members of a marketing "staff" you did not even know you had.

Conclusion

As you may have gathered from the pages of this chapter, museum marketers have literally hundreds of tools at their disposal for promoting their organizations using any number of dynamic and unique marketing strategies that fit into any budget. The one essential marketing tool you cannot be without is fortunately plentiful and free of cost: the enthusiasm that you devote to your museum and the desire to showcase it to an eager public. Your organization is the steward of an amazing legacy and a priceless collection, and your accomplishments, your partners, and your mission are of inestimable value to your community. Your museum needs your passion to convey its purpose exuberantly and to draw generations of visitors who will support it for years to come. Marketing connects your museum's legacy to its audience, and the enthusiasm that you bring to your marketing makes the legacy worth sharing.

Resources

Beckwith, Harry. *The Invisible Touch: The Four Keys to Modern Marketing*. New York: Warner Books, Inc., 2000.

Bernoff, Josh, and Charlene Li. *Groundswell: Winning in a World Transformed by Social Technologies*. Boston: Harvard Business Press, 2008.

Brooks, Roger A., and Maury Forman. *Your Town, a Destination: The 25 Immutable Rules of Successful Tourism*. 2nd ed. Olympia, WA: Destination Development, Inc., 2006.

Godin, Seth. *Unleashing the Ideavirus*. Dobbs Ferry, NY: Do You Zoom Inc., 2000.

Halligan, Brian, and Dharmesh Shah. *Inbound Marketing: Get Found Using Google, Social Media, and Blogs*. Hoboken, NJ: John Wiley & Sons, 2010.

Museum Next. www.museummarketing.co.uk (accessed May 30, 2011).

Scott, David Meerman. *The New Rules of Marketing and PR: How to Use Social Media, Blogs, News Releases, Online Video, and Viral Marketing to Reach Buyers Directly*. 2nd ed. Hoboken, NJ: John Wiley & Sons, 2010.

Shaping Outcomes: Making a Difference in Libraries and Museums. www.shaping outcomes.org (accessed May 30, 2011).

Simon, Nina. Museum 2.0. www.museumtwo.blogspot.com (accessed May 30, 2011).

Notes

1. Amy Stark, *The 2009 Tweeter's Almanac First Edition: The Great #Indiana Initiative of Aught Nine* (Carmel, IN: Stark ReAlity Enterprises), 46. Available at http://bit.ly/swFYI (accessed May 30, 2011).

2. Ben McConnell and Jackie Huba, *Citizen Marketers: When People Are the Message* (Chicago: Kaplan Press, 2007).

3. "DMO General Information," Destination Marketing Association International, Resource Center, www.destinationmarketing.org/resource_center (accessed January 18, 2011).

4. "Introduction to the Advertising and Branding Industry," Plunkett Research Ltd., www.plunkettresearch.com/Industries/AdvertisingandBranding (accessed January 21, 2011).

5. "Travel Facts and Statistics," U.S. Travel Association, http://www.ustravel.org/news/press-kit/travel-facts-and-statistics (accessed September 21, 2011).

6. Ki Mae Heussne, "Is Facebook Aging Gracefully?" ABC News, http://abcnews.go.com/Technology/AheadoftheCurve/story?id=8044711&page=1 (accessed January 29, 2011).

CHAPTER TWO

IN LIEU OF MIND READING:
VISITOR STUDIES AND EVALUATION[1]
Stacy Klingler and Conny Graft

If we could read minds, we would know exactly what exhibits to show next
year, what programs should accompany them, and how much text on a label
is too much, too little, or just right. We could know what hours to be open
so that the most people would come. We would understand what topics appeal
to teenagers, moms with young children, fathers who work the swing shift, and
visitors from out of town. Unfortunately, we cannot read minds. We can best determine the contents of the hearts and minds of those people who choose to visit
us—and, if we make the effort to find them, those who do not—by conducting
visitor studies and evaluations. If we ask our visitors what they think about what
we do, and sometimes if we watch them use our museum, we can find some
clues that will help us make good choices about exhibit topics, program formats,
museum hours, and more.

Oh no, you are saying to yourself. One more thing I have to learn? How am
I supposed to find time to ask people what they think about our activities when
I barely have time to take care of the collection, put up new exhibits, spread the
word about our upcoming programs, pay the bills, raise money to pay the bills,
and keep the bathroom clean? When you are running a small museum, your job
is to juggle all these tasks (and more), and you are working just to keep the balls
in the air. Can you really add one more?

Yes! Because that ball is going to help you decide which balls you really
need to keep in the air and which you can set aside. The key to success is setting
priorities—knowing which balls to juggle. And visitor studies and evaluation can
help you make those decisions in a way that makes your institution more relevant, more appealing, and more valued by your visitors. It is not a silver bullet,
and it does not enable you to read minds, but it will give you insight into how
to improve what you do for your visitors. It may very well make your current job
a lot easier!

Visitor studies and evaluation tell us specifically about our programs, exhibits, facilities, and the like. We ask about how we stack up against a set of criteria

37

either set by the visitors (are the bathrooms clean enough? did I enjoy my visit?) or determined internally in goals and outcomes set by the board or staff for the institution, an exhibit, or a program (did the visitors understand the theme of the exhibit? did we bring in more young adults with this program?). Evaluation can (and should) happen at many points in the process of creating an exhibit, publication, program, or other activity. We tend to think of evaluation only at the end of a project. However, you can use it at the beginning of the process (e.g., by asking visitors about the major subtopics in an exhibit or their knowledge of a topic) or during the middle (e.g., by testing out an interactive component of a program with a few visitors). Like visitor studies, good evaluations help us make decisions, either in modifying a current course of action (e.g., deciding what elements should be a part of an exhibit) or in making plans for the future (e.g., deciding if we should do a similar program again).

Collecting Information about Your Visitors

If you are not already collecting information about who is visiting you, gathering basic demographic information may be the best place to start conducting visitor studies. Finding out who is actually coming to your museum helps you know who you are reaching and who you are not. By combining this basic demographic information with a few questions or observations of visitors, you can begin to go beyond understanding who is coming to gathering information about how to serve your visitors better.

You can gather demographic information either by asking people to categorize themselves when signing your visitor register or you can ask docents or greeters to keep a tally sheet. You will get the most accurate information by asking the visitors to categorize themselves. However, provided your greeters are trained (more on this later), you can ask them to categorize visitors, and then you will have a record for close to 100 percent of people who come through your doors.

If you use the categories for age, income, race, and education collected by the U.S. census, you can compare your visitors with your community to see how well you are reaching different demographics. For example, Conny Graft lives in James City County, Virginia, and when she went to the U.S. Census Bureau website and looked up demographics for her county, she discovered the information in table 2.1.

If Graft were to conduct a visitor study at a museum that serves people in her county, she would use the same categories for gender, age, and race used in the census survey for people to check off on her survey. Visit the U.S. Census Bureau website to find demographic information for your community.[2]

Table 2.1. U.S. Census (2000) Profile of General Demographic Characteristics for James City County, Virginia[1]

	Number	Percent
Total population	48,102	100.0
Sex		
Male	23,294	48.4
Female	24,808	51.6
Age		
Under five years	2,709	5.6
Five to nine years	3,169	6.6
Ten to fourteen years	3,376	7.0
Fifteen to nineteen years	2,838	5.9
Twenty to twenty-four years	2,211	4.6
Twenty-five to thirty-four years	5,273	11.0
Thirty-five to forty-four years	7,866	16.4
Forty-five to fifty-four years	7,043	14.6
Fifty-five to fifty-nine years	2,931	6.1
Sixty to sixty-four years	2,589	5.4
Sixty-five to seventy-four years	4,591	9.5
Seventy-five to eighty-four years	2,628	5.5
Eighty-five years and over	878	1.8
Race		
One race	47,448	98.6
White	39,467	82.0
Black or African American	6,910	14.4
American Indian and Alaska Native	134	0.3
Asian	702	1.5
Asian Indian	100	0.2
Chinese	151	0.3
Filipino	163	0.3
Japanese	55	0.1
Korean	159	0.3
Vietnamese	27	0.1
Other Asian	47	0.1
Native Hawaiian and Other Pacific Islander	22	0.0
Native Hawaiian	12	0.0
Guamanian or Chamorro	3	0.0
Samoan	5	0.0
Other Pacific Islander[2]	2	0.0
Some other race	213	0.4
Two or more races	654	1.4

[1]"DP-1. Profile of General Demographic Characteristics: 2000; Data Set: Census 2000 Summary File 1 (SF 1) 100-Percent Data; Geographic Area: James City County, Virginia," U.S. Census Department, http://factfinder.census.gov/servlet/QT-Table?_bm=n&_lang=en&qr_name=DEC_2000_SF1_U_DP1&ds_name=DEC_2000_SF1_U&geo_id=05000US51095 (accessed May 31, 2011).

Note: The table above reports an estimate taken from data collected between 2000 and 2009. Data for 2010 is currently being downloaded as of this printing, state by state, beginning May 2011.

TEXTBOX 2.1

EVALUATION SEEMS SCARY

Evaluation can be intimidating. It is feedback on what you are doing, and who wants to find out that they are doing a bad job? Evaluation might remind you of school grades or performance evaluations at work that affect your job security. If you depend largely on volunteers, you may be afraid that evaluating your activities may scare your valuable human resources away. And this may be true if the people in your group are unwilling or unable to change. There is no point to evaluating what you do if you aren't willing to act on what you find.

But take heart! Most people who care about what they do would like to do it better. Most people would like to see more people spending more time enjoying your museum and all it has to offer. And although we can frequently make improvement through internal conversations about what did and did not work, ultimately everything we do—from caring for collections to raising money and from researching a newsletter article to hosting a visiting speaker—we do for the public, for our audience. What they think must matter if we are going to do a good job of serving them. Finding out what they think should not be an afterthought.

If you take the time to explain your plans for evaluation to paid and unpaid staff and the board in this way, you are more likely to get their cooperation in collecting information and implementing change.

You might introduce your evaluation plans to those who will be affected in a small group and make the following items part of your meeting:

- Ask people to share past evaluation experiences, be they either positive or negative.
- Acknowledge that evaluation can feel a little scary or like a waste of time.
- Explain how you intend to report on and use the information (to make global changes, not to pick on anyone in particular).
- Remind them that this is a learning process for you too and that the first attempts will not be perfect and that you will need their feedback.
- Most importantly, let them know it is not a performance appraisal.

Making the Case for Visitor Studies and Evaluation

Once you have decided that visitor studies and evaluation are important enough to add a new ball to the five (or seven or twelve) that you are juggling as the leader of a small museum, you will probably have to convince others (paid or unpaid staff and board members) that collecting information about who your visitors are and what they think about your museum is important. Here are some arguments you may want to make:

- *For the money-minded board member:* Potential funders want to know about our visitors. Federal granting agencies for many years have required basic demographic information about whom museums serve as part of the grant application process. State and local funding sources are beginning to ask for that information more and more. Private foundations also want to be sure that their money is making a difference and will ask you how you will evaluate the success of your efforts. If we want to ask the county tourism bureau for funding, real numbers about who is visiting from outside of the county will help us demonstrate our impact on tourism.

- *For the efficiency expert:* By investing a little time and money now, we will have more information that will help us allocate time and money better. Why? Because we will know more about whom we are and are not serving and where we should be focusing current dollars and time.

- *For the museum content lover (e.g., history, art, geology):* Our mission, ultimately, is to get people to care about and learn from our subject. As we compete for attention with work, school, sports, pop culture, television, and the latest Internet craze, we need to know how and where we can connect with our current visitors and potential visitors and what will engage them with our topic. This information will help us better articulate and pursue our mission and our reason for being.

- *For the civic-minded community booster:* Asking our visitors about what they think and value is a way of showing we care about them. It can also help us identify potential visitors who may not be aware of our programs and services.

- *For the person who says we never do anything:* Visitor studies and evaluation provide the evidence we need to shake us loose from the status quo. How will those people who say, "We've always done it this way," argue when the information is coming from the horse's mouth—from our visitors?

- *For the director:* Finding out who your visitors are and what they think about your museum can help you determine which balls are most important to juggle. That in turn can help all staff and volunteers keep their eyes on these key activities. By following the steps of planning an evaluation, you as director, together with board members, staff, and volunteers, will also be forced to define and articulate what you want visitors to know, feel, and do as a result of a visit to the museum.

By making these arguments, you can work to convince your board and all the people, paid and unpaid, who work in the museum that your organization should spend some time finding out about its visitors. However, you might be working with someone who simply does not see why you cannot just knock out this project in an afternoon by "walking the floor" and talking with people in the museum. Why make a big production out of what you can do with a comment card or a conversation? What is the value of "visitor studies"?

Doing It Right: Ensuring Validity and Reliability

What makes visitor studies or evaluation different from more informal ways that we might get feedback about what we do? The short answer is that it uses scientific protocols, and in doing so, it can ensure that the information you collect is valid and reliable.

Reliability is about measuring something consistently. If the answers to your questions change based on who is asking them or because the questions themselves are changing, then your information is not reliable or useful. *Validity* is about measuring what you intend to measure. If you are trying to measure interest by tracking how long people look at exhibits, but people look longer at exhibits with benches near them, you are not actually measuring interest, and your study is not valid.

To be reliable and valid, protocols are systematic, both in whom you ask questions of and how you seek the information. When you walk the floor, you get information from certain types of people: people who are comfortable sharing their opinions, people who are not in a hurry, people who look you in the eye as you scan the room, and probably people who look like you. We are most comfortable talking to people who are similar to us and look like they want to talk to us. But they represent only a subset of your visitors. What about the people who are not having a good time? What about those who are more introverted? When you walk the floor, you also may ask your questions in different ways that lead to different answers.

When you do not develop questions in advance and ask them the same way every time, you might try to steer people to where you have recently invested time and money, or your own opinions might creep in.

By following protocols, you will get information from a broad group of people, not just the extroverts and the complainers. You avoid the problem of the squeaky wheel getting the grease. Just because someone has an opinion and is quite happy to share it does not mean that he or she speaks for all your visitors. Protocols help you create a neutral space for your visitors to share their opinions; they also help you reduce the biases that the questioner may bring to the conversation and ensure that you get a representative sample.

Using Random Sample Selection

If you are not able to ask questions of every single person who visits your museum or exhibit, then you need to collect information from a sample of your visitors. To ensure that the sample of respondents is similar to the larger group of visitors to your museum, you need to use random sample selection, which means that you ask every third person who passes a specific location in the museum or exhibit your questions. It could be that you ask every other person or every fourth or fifth person. The spot passed could be a bench or a doorway. The important thing is to pick a number and a landmark and to stick with your system. Otherwise, you will end up asking friendly people who look like you. When you use random sample selection, you will discover that the characteristics of the people you talked to (such as age, sex, education, income, number of visits) will be representative of the entire group of visitors that comes to your museum. This is called a representative sample. If you must select a group to represent a larger group (as in a focus group), read about good methods for choosing participants in Judy Diamond's *Practical Evaluation Guide: Tools for Museums and Other Informal Educational Settings* or Judith Sharken Simon's *The Wilder Nonprofit Field Guide to Conducting Successful Focus Groups* (see "Getting Started Resources" at the end of the chapter).

Visitor Studies and Evaluation As a Way of Life

Visitor studies and evaluation form a process that, ideally, you will incorporate into all the activities of your organization. The next section provides a step-by-step plan for the process, but your long-term goal should be to ingrain this way of thinking and acting into how you operate. Whether planning a new exhibit, creating a new program, or revamping a website, you need to consider getting input from your visitors as automatically as you think about how you will use your collection, who will present that new program, or what content should be included.

Conducting good visitor studies takes time and effort. In the ideal situation—one with a board friendly to the idea of evaluation—a board member or staff person would present the benefits of evaluation to the board with a proposal or request to devote time and resources to a project. However, if the board seems unlikely to support a formal proposal, build evaluation into an upcoming project, recognizing, as the paid or unpaid staff person, that you need to include some extra time to do it.

Following the section on process, this chapter provides a brief overview of the types of methods that exist and the pros and cons of each. It is beyond the scope of this chapter to provide in-depth information about how to complete each type of study. Please see the resource list at the end of the chapter to determine what additional reading you might want to do. Additionally, we highly recommend you contact a local university (start with the education, psychology, or business department) or small marketing research business to request some pro bono consulting. Professors are often looking for real-world projects to give their students, and this will provide you with wonderful expertise at no cost. Taking someone with experience in social science or marketing research out for a lunch meeting may yield some advice on methods or even an offer of assistance.

When you use the tools of visitor studies and evaluation regularly, you bring clarity to your institution, mission, and programs because doing so forces you to define clearly what you want visitors to get out of the experience. It also helps you better meet your visitors' needs because you have been thinking and asking about them as a part of the planning process. The process is really common sense, formalized in a way that keeps our biases in check. First, we define the goals of an experience, exhibit, or program. Next, we decide what information will be most helpful in making key decisions about it. Then, we figure out what questions and tools from the visitor studies and evaluation toolkit will help us get at that information most effectively (and within our budget and time constraints). Finally, we gather and analyze the data, decide what it tells us, and put it to good use.

What's the Process?

Once visitor studies and evaluation are a part of your process, they are relatively easy to sustain because you get hungry for the information. But getting the ball rolling can be daunting. This section provides a step-by-step plan to jump-start the process (see table 2.2 for a summary).

PUTTING IT ALL TOGETHER AT THE BELFAST HISTORICAL SOCIETY AND MUSEUM

The Belfast Historical Society and Museum is an all-volunteer organization dedicated to the collection, conservation, preservation, and interpretation of artifacts relevant to Belfast, Maine. The society operates a museum and archive in a historic home for five months of the year with two summer interns on a budget of less than $30,000 per year.

The board began with a question: How might we serve our local community better and raise our profile in the community? In 2008, as part of the pilot testing of the Standards and Excellence Program for History Organizations, the society picked visitor and audience research as an area that could help it answer this question.

From its guest register, the society asked its student interns to tally where visitors were coming from. They discovered that the museum's largest audience was tourists instead of locals. Board members identified improving their relationship with the local audience, including both school groups and adult visitors, as the top priority.

The next step was to get training on how to conduct various types of studies. Through the New England Museum Association, the society located a qualified museum professional with visitor studies experience who provided a three-hour training session for two summer interns, the board president, the archivist, and another board member. The $180 fee for the training was the most expensive part of the research efforts, but it provided the group with a solid understanding of visitor research and helped them decide what methods to use to gather information. Additionally, they purchased Judy Diamond's *Practical Evaluation Guide*, and two team members read it from cover to cover.

Because they wanted a broad picture and to be sure of what they found before investing in changes, they chose multiple methods for gathering data: written questionnaires, interviews, observations, and focus groups.

Focus groups
They conducted three focus groups with local adults (visitors and nonvisitors), community leaders, and students. This information proved to be the most useful in the short term, in part because the act of asking helped

(continued)

improve community relations and because the groups offered concrete suggestions for change. Each group spent one hour reviewing the museum and
then participated in a roundtable discussion led by an experienced outside
facilitator, either from another museum or the University of Maine. From
the local adult group, they learned that locals were interested in the local
economic history and more recent history. (The group also served to culti-
vate some artifact donors.) From the community leaders, they learned that
their signage was insufficient, the exterior of building was not as attractive
as it could be, and the entry area needed to be more welcoming. From the
students, they learned how little local history was understood and that the
students were interested in the clothing displays, notable Belfast people, and
Belfast education but not the Civil War or ship models. They found that
this was the most useful form of research because it provided unexpected
information as well as developed community relationships.

Interviews
Summer interns and board members completed twelve interviews with
interested visitors using scripted, open-ended questions. These interviews
provided in-depth information about what interested museum visitors and
how well they were serving those visitors. These were the most challenging
to complete, as they required a lot of volunteer or intern time.

Observations
Interns and docents informally tracked the amount of time visitors spent
looking at various displays. The observations corroborated what the interviews and student focus group revealed about which displays were more
interesting: "Notable Women of Belfast" was studied by all types of people
(men/women, young/old), yet many walked past what many board members
believed to be a magnificent ship model and a key railroad exhibit.

Questionnaires
Over a four-month period, they gathered written questionnaires from museum visitors (generally tourists) and from special event attendees (generally locals). From the responses, they discovered what visitors liked about
museum, the overall audience demographics, what people knew about the
museum, and why they visited.

Based on the results of these varied research methods, the board has made
substantial changes that have improved the museum's relationship with
schools and the local audience. Belfast residents have been pleased by modi-

fications to signage, the building exterior, and the entryway. The elementary and middle schools now invite the society to help teach local history, and a reliable stream of summer interns comes from the high school.

The information collected has not always provided a clear picture. Some feedback has indicated that exhibit labels are overwhelming and cluttered; other feedback reveals that visitors appreciate the depth of information on the labels. Their studies have indicated that exhibits related to the shipping industry are not of great interest, but that piece of history is essential to the Belfast story. What are the next steps? The society intends to do more focus groups to help it better understand how to engage its various audiences. While it continues to collect the written surveys, the group plans for more interviews and focus groups to provide more in-depth ideas and direction.

The process of learning about and doing visitor research changed the mind-set of the board. It has created a written policy and plan for ongoing institutional evaluation and an evaluation manual that puts visitors at the center of the society's efforts for progress. Although it does not have the resources to make every change that the research suggests, the audience feedback has provided much of the direction for the organization's five-year plan and the priorities that it will pursue far into the future.

Step 1: Pick a Project

Start Small

Just about any activity of an organization can benefit from evaluation information, but that does not mean that you should start by evaluating everything. Pick an event, program, or small exhibit as a starting point. Focusing on a single, time-limited activity will help narrow the scope and make the first project more manageable. If you are doing the very first evaluation for your institution, starting with a small event or program will help you reach your most important internal goal, which is to get the board, staff, and volunteers on board to do more visitor studies and find out more about visitors.

Choose a Leader

You may have some flexibility about who takes the lead on the project. While evaluation is a very reasonable project for a paid staff member, and presumably a paid staff member would be quite interested in the results, starting the evaluation process can be a good project for a dedicated volunteer or intern. The evaluation leader must be willing to understand evaluation methods, to learn by doing (trial and error), and to listen. The role might be a great fit for someone who would

STARTING SMALL

When you start small and ask questions whose answers you know you can use right away, you can demonstrate the value of visitor studies to your board, staff, and volunteers without much cost to the organization.

When Stacy Klingler started as the director of the Putnam County Museum in Greencastle, Indiana, the museum was just one year old. From the standard guest book visitor register (which asks for date, name, and address), she knew that 203 people visited in the first year during the opening hours of 1 p.m. to 6 p.m. on Thursdays.

To provide information the board wanted for making decisions (such as when to be open and how people were learning about the museum), she replaced the standard guest book. She created a very short form printed on loose-leaf paper and set out in a three-ring binder. Visitors could still page back to see who had visited (as they frequently did with the guest book), but she was able to ask a few additional questions and to modify those questions easily over time.

In the first iteration, the visitor register asked

- name
- city/state (listed before address to separate it from the possibility of getting an unwanted mailing)
- address (noting that this was optional)
- date and time of visit (with a small calendar and clock on display next to the binder)
- how visitor heard about the museum (with the options of friend, newspaper, poster, and other)

The answers were summarized monthly using an Excel spreadsheet and reported to the board. After a year, they had some great information. With the city/state data, they were able to tell the county visitors' bureau that 14 percent of visitors came from out of the county. With the date and time information, they were able to show how much of their increased visitation was during new hours—10 a.m. to 4 p.m. on Saturdays—and how many visitors came on days they were not officially open, thus demonstrating the need for expanded hours and additional staff. They were also able to determine that the late hours on Thursday were ineffective: In one year, just one person had visited between 5 p.m. and 6 p.m. Later iterations added questions about the number of people in a visiting group, whether the visitor had visited before, and whether the visitor was a member.

You can be even more informal and flexible with your initial research efforts. Consider asking just a single question, as the Scottsburg Heritage Center in Scottsburg, Indiana, did. When visitors entered, the docent asked, "How did you find out about the museum?" and tallied the answer on a piece of paper. This question revealed that the radio public service announcements were a very effective means of reaching people. A few months later, the docent asked, "Did you come to see something in particular today?" The answers to this question revealed which of their marketing efforts were more successful in bringing people in. (Special temporary exhibits were a driver of attendance.)

You can choose to ask a question at any point in a visit, as long as you ask the same question of every visitor and have a simple way of recording answers. If your question is very open-ended, you might simply record the answers in a notebook and then tally the answers into meaningful categories on a regular basis. For example, if you ask at the end of the visit, "What was the most interesting thing you learned today?" you might find a pattern about which exhibits are attracting visitors' attention. This might lead you to do more in-depth research to determine if the topic or story is the compelling force or the manner of display or storytelling makes the difference.

As you grow more comfortable with asking questions, you may decide to ask a few questions of each visitor. Remember, visitor studies do not have to be complicated. It only needs to focus on information you can and will use and to be systematic—ask each and every visitor and ask the same question of everyone.

---

like to do a project mostly outside of business hours, as most of the planning and analyzing need not be done on-site. The leader should be comfortable with managing data, either in paper or electronic form, and could be a good fit for a retired teacher or a college faculty member (or spouse).

Include Stakeholders

Who else should be involved in the evaluation process? Staff, volunteers, and community members are likely candidates. One of the best ways to keep people who might feel threatened by the evaluation (those whose work you might be perceived to be evaluating) from writing off the results is to involve them early in the process. You might also want to include representatives from the target audience in some way.

Think about how you involve stakeholders in the evaluation process. Should they help define outcomes (step 2)? Should they be involved in drafting questions (step 8)? Will you include them in a meeting to discuss your findings (step 10)? Stakeholders who may have to make changes as a result of a study will be more open to them if they have been involved in planning the evaluation. This does not mean that all stakeholders who have been involved will jump up and yell, "Oh wow! Let's make changes!" but they may be encouraged to think differently about the program or exhibit you are evaluating.

Step 2: Define Desired Outcomes

Draft outcome statements for your program, exhibit, or other museum experience. What do you want guests to *know*, *feel*, and *do*, both during and after their experience? The outcomes need to be mission related, meaningful, and measurable. Here is an example of possible outcomes for a tour of the White House:

- *Know (cognitive outcome):* After a tour of the White House, 65 percent of guests will have a greater understanding of how the role of the president has changed over time.
- *Feel (affective outcome):* During the tour of the White House, 65 percent of guests will feel an increased appreciation for the role of the president.
- *Do (behavioral outcome):* After the tour of the White House, 55 percent of guests will vote in their next local, state, or federal election.

Now draft outcome statements for what you want your visitors to know, feel, and do during and after an experience at your museum. Then draft outcome statements reflecting what you think your visitors hope for from your program, exhibit, or museum. Do they want to learn something new, enjoy a social outing with friends, have fun with their families, or share stories they have about the history of the area? While you may not have data at this point that tells you what visitors or potential visitors want, make a list of your assumptions about what you think they want and then test these assumptions with a survey.

Step 3: Define the Target Audience

Determine whom you want to come to this program, exhibit, or museum: Is it schoolchildren, families with children, or vacationing retirees? Your target audience will shape the methods you use. For example, you probably will not have kids who visit on a field trip fill out an online survey, and you probably will not invite an out-of-town visitor to a focus group next month. Having a specific

CASE STUDY: OUTCOME-BASED PLANNING AND EVALUATION AT THE McLEAN COUNTY MUSEUM OF HISTORY

Evaluation in museums, particularly evaluation of educational programs and exhibits, is moving in the direction of outcome-based evaluation. This type of evaluation is increasingly required for national grants (such as those from the Institute of Museum and Library Services) and will likely be requested by state and foundation funders more and more.

Outcome-based evaluation goes beyond gathering information about how many people participate in a program or like an exhibit; its goal is to measure how the programs or exhibits change the participant. Outcomes are measured in terms of what people know, feel, think, or do after experiencing your activity. We frequently evaluate our efforts based on outputs—counting what services or activities we have offered or created as the measure of success. Measuring outcomes requires you to think about and gather information not simply about your activities but about the people you are trying to serve.

This evaluation system also directs you to think about evaluation and outcomes in the planning stages of the project rather than at the end. It uses a logic model to guide planning efforts to examine the resources needed for a project (inputs), the step-by-step tasks (activities), the things produced (outputs), the measurable changes in the audience (outcomes), and the long-term goals that guide the project. (For an example of a logic model, see table 1.1 in chapter 1 in this book.) By examining the project from beginning to end and with outputs, outcome, and goals in mind, the logic model guides both planning and evaluation efforts.

At the McLean County Museum of History in Bloomington, Illinois, museum staff members measure the outcome of learning in the students who participate in classroom presentations. To evaluate the outcomes, teachers administer a four-question pretest and posttest for each presentation that measures specific content knowledge covered in the activities. By measuring each student's knowledge before and after the program, the staff can calculate how much knowledge each student gained that day and show the average knowledge gained per student. This outcome is distinct from the number of students who participate (an output) or the long-term goal of the program (to engage students in history through hands-on activities and artifacts).

(continued)

Outcome-based evaluation comes from the education field, and there has been some debate about how the focus on measurable changes in visitors may hamper creativity and richness in museums, particularly in exhibits.[1] However, as with other evaluation efforts, once you build thinking about outcomes in as part of the process, doing so becomes second nature and provides you with valuable data to demonstrate the power of your efforts to impact your visitors.

Note

1. Andrew J. Pekarik, "From Knowing to Not Knowing: Moving beyond 'Outcomes,'" *Curator: The Museum Journal* 53, no. 1 (January 2010): 105–15.

audience in mind also may help you make decisions about marketing and the content and structure of the program, exhibit, or museum itself.

Step 4: Define What You Need to Know

Reviewing the list of outcomes you developed in step 2, make a list of the types of things you need to know. For example: We need to know if the program is meeting the outcomes that we want. We also need to know if our assumptions about what visitors want from this experience are correct. We want to know basic demographics about the visitors who come and how they heard about the program, exhibit, or museum. This is not a list of the actual questions you will be asking visitors. It is a list of the types of information you hope the study will provide answers for.

Now, take the top four or five things you need to know and list how you will use the data from each of those items to make decisions about the program, exhibit, or museum. It is very easy to collect data but very hard to collect data that will actually be used. We sometimes want to know something just because it would be interesting. You do not want to ask visitors for their time for mere intellectual curiosity—you want their donation of time to have a real impact on the choices you make.

In choosing questions and topics to investigate, the evaluation leader should ask, "If we had the answer to this question, how would we use that information to make a decision?" If the answer is that the results could not be used to make a decision about the program or service, then that question or topic should be

AUDIENCE

Sometimes you will see the word "audience" appear instead of "visitor," especially as you read other studies and research. Your audience is the people you would like to have visit, regardless of whether they actually have contact with you. In the words of the American Association for State and Local History's Standards and Excellence Program for History Organizations, your audience comprises "the people for whom the institution designs and delivers messages, programs and services."[1]

Visitors are the people who actually enter your doors, attended a program, or visit your website. For most small museums, visitors and audiences are the same people. The people you intend to serve are the ones who actually visit and vice versa.

We sometimes break up that idea of audience into subgroups so that we can focus on getting different groups interested in the museum or serving them in a better way. You might divide your audience into groups based on demographic information (age, gender, race, ethnicity), based on how they visit your museum (adult tours, school field trips, intergeneration family visits, in couples, in small groups, alone, or on the website), or based on interest (antiques, sports, cars). Your neighbors are also an audience worth considering. Simply by their proximity to your museum, the people who live and work nearby are affected by your activities.

To explore more about the differences between visitors and audiences, read the *Museum Audience Insight* blog.[2]

Notes
1. "Glossary," *StEPs Workbook* (Nashville, TN: AASLH, 2009), 313.
2. Susie Wilkening, "Visitors? Or Audiences? Or Both?" Museum Audience Insight, August 10, 2010, http://reachadvisors.typepad.com/museum_audience_insight/2010/08/visitors-or-audiences-or-both.html (accessed January 17, 2011.)

eliminated. For example, do not ask your visitors if an evening program would be better than a lunch program if the organization cannot staff an evening event. Do not ask about adding interactive activities to an exhibit if the organization will not allocate the time or funds to make the addition. As your organization grows more comfortable with the insights visitor studies provide, you can begin to tackle questions that may be more controversial.

Step 5: Review Current Information

Even if your organization has never done formal evaluation, you may have access to material that will help give you direction. Do you have comments in your visitor registers that may provide insight? Are there any comment cards about the topic? Does anyone have anecdotal information or observations from past activities that may help narrow your questions? Have you looked at comments visitors have made about your museum on Trip Advisor, Yelp, Yahoo! Travel, Virtual Tourist, and other travel review sites?

You might even survey your staff, volunteers, and board members about what they hear from visitors. All people who work at the museum, including housekeepers and greeters, have been collecting visitor responses for years. Allowing them to express what they see and hear day in and day out will assist you in understanding some of the visitor data you are collecting. It will also help communicate to your staff and volunteers that their voices are important as well. While these resources do not represent the systematic and unbiased collection of information, they certainly provide clues for where to begin.

You will also want to look for visitor studies and audience research information related to your topic from other organizations or the museum, education, or tourism fields in general (see the "Visitor Research Databases" resource section at the end of the chapter for websites where you can find this information). Also contact your local chamber of commerce and tourism board to see if they have collected information about people who live in your area or have visited your site.

Step 6: Choose the Type(s) of Evaluation You Will Do

During the course of a project, the point at which you choose to do the evaluation depends on what you want to know and when you need to know it. *Front-end evaluation* happens at the beginning, while the program or exhibit is still being defined. We know, for example, that learning involves making connections between what one already knows and new information about a subject. Front-end evaluation is very useful for finding out what visitors know about the history of a topic and theme before they enter your program, exhibit, or museum. Then, when you begin to craft your exhibit or program, you can start with what visitors are already familiar with so that they can connect to the new information you are presenting. *Formative evaluation* or *prototyping*, during which a cheaper or partial version of the exhibit or program is evaluated, happens early in the process. This type of evaluation allows you to test out different types of labels, signs, displays, or live interpretive methods with small groups of visitors so that you can make mistakes before you invest heavily in more expensive exhibit materials or staff training. It is also a great type of evaluation to use when you and your team cannot decide which design or interpretive technique will be most effective. It allows you to spend less time debating the pros and cons of an idea. *Remedial evaluation* happens while the activity (usually an exhibit) is going on and is used to troubleshoot and make modifications to things like lighting, crowd flow, signs, and so forth. *Summative evaluation* happens at the end of the process to produce "lessons learned" for the next similar activity.

Step 7: Choose the Methods You Will Use

What evaluation method(s) will you use and why? Will you conduct a survey, perform an observation, or use a focus group? The section "Methods: Pros and Cons," together with your other reading or training, will help you make these decisions.

Step 8: Write Your Questions

Writing questions is one of the most challenging parts of visitor studies. Getting assistance from experienced researchers can help you save time and ensure both that the data you collect is linked to the list of things you need to know and that the wording is not biased. It is also critical that you test your survey and questions with actual visitors several times. You will find yourself rewriting your questions multiple times. You will also want to consider how much time you are asking for from your participants. Unless you are conducting a focus group or prearranged interview, you will probably want to keep the time commitment to less than fifteen minutes.

Step 9: Give It a Try—Collect Data

You will never have the perfect set of survey questions, focus group prompts, or observational coding systems. So, take a stab and learn as you go. If you are working with a group of volunteers to collect the information, be sure to take the time to train them so that they understand the hows and whys of the process. Gather your information, keeping notes about what does and does not seem to be working and what you might do differently next time.

One other tip: Before you collect your data, give the questions to your volunteers, staff, and board members, and ask them to tell you what they think the results will be from the visitors. Then, when you share the actual visitor results, compare them to the staff, volunteer, and board member predictions to uncover any gaps. Identifying, understanding, and managing the gap between what these stakeholders think visitors want and learn and what visitors actually want and learn is critical to long-term success.

RECRUITING AND TRAINING VOLUNTEERS AND STAFF TO CONDUCT SURVEYS

Asking volunteers or staff to approach visitors and conduct a survey sounds fairly easy—and it is. But there are some key steps you should follow to ensure the process goes smoothly.

Recruiting

Conny Graft has had many years of experience recruiting volunteers to conduct surveys at both Colonial Williamsburg and at other historic sites. For her, the most critical aspect begins with recruiting. Not everyone is suited for conducting surveys. When recruiting volunteers, she looks for five key things in a volunteer or staff person: Is he or she (1) an active listener, (2) hospitable and courteous, (3) knowledgeable about the museum, (4) unafraid to approach strangers, and (5) excited about doing surveys? When she recruits people to conduct surveys, she lets volunteers know that after they are trained and conduct a survey, they may find it is not for them. If that is the case, they can opt out of the project.

Training

The next critical step is obtaining training. Your first job is to train yourself. In addition to reading this book and reading some of the literature in the "Resources" section, Graft recommends that you find a professional from your state field services office (see www.aaslh.org/FSA/FSA.html to find a directory of field services offices by state) or a professor in a nearby college to show you how to conduct a survey. At the very least, you need to get out on the floor and conduct several surveys before you train someone else in how to do it.

Key Things Volunteers and Staff Need To Do Before Conducting a Survey

1. Understand the purpose of the survey and how it will help the museum
2. Understand how to use random sample selection (every third person who walks by a specific landmark or every first visitor) in selecting visitors to do the survey
3. Familiarize themselves with all the questions on the survey
4. Practice making eye contact with the visitor they are approaching
5. Rehearse keeping the invitation brief
6. After completing the survey, go to a quiet corner and review and rewrite notes if necessary

Approaching Visitors

Graft tells staff and volunteers to begin by offering assistance to the visitor: "Hi, my name is Conny and I work/volunteer here at the museum. Do you have any questions about this museum or exhibit I can help you with?" Offering visitor assistance first will allow you to establish a relationship with them before you ask for their help.

Then make the actual invitation *very brief*: "We are talking with visitors like you today about their experiences in this museum to help us improve our services. This survey will only take five to ten minutes." Pause and wait for visitors' response. While you have not actually asked them to take a survey, this is implied. If they say no, thank them and then move on to your next visitor. If they say yes, be ready to suggest other things the other guests in the travel party can do while you are conducting the survey. If the other members want to listen in on the survey, that is fine too. If a spouse or friend begins to interrupt the other person or starts offering answers, just say, "That's interesting, but I have been instructed to only record one person's answers."

Practice, Practice, Practice

Graft then meets with each volunteer separately and shows him or her how she approaches visitors and conducts the survey. She conducts one or two surveys while the volunteer observes, and then she observes the volunteer conducting about three surveys and gives feedback. This is the best time to correct any issues that may arise before bad habits are adopted. If the staff member or volunteer is not successful in getting visitors to conduct a survey, review several factors to see what might be causing this to happen. Was the invitation brief? Did she or he make eye contact? Did she or he offer to help the visitor first?

Picking a Location

If you find that people are refusing to participate, location may also be an issue. There is no one magic spot to conduct a survey. Is this location either too close to the entrance or the exit? If you are doing front-end evaluation, and you want to know what people know about a topic before you plan the exhibit or program, then you can conduct the survey outside a local coffee shop or library or with visitors after they have just entered the museum. If you want feedback on an exhibit or program after they have seen it, then you need to select a location near the exit. If you are surveying visitors about a house tour, conduct the survey outside (weather permitting) so that you do not hold up the touring schedule. Consider trying other locations if you are not getting the participation you would like.

(continued)

TEXTBOX 2.6 (*Continued*)

Expressing Appreciation
Review the surveys after each day, and follow up with the volunteers to thank them for their work and to address any questions that they or you may have about some of the responses. Be sure to share the results with them after all surveys have been completed and include a special thank-you to each volunteer in any report that is written about the survey.

Step 10: Analyze, Share, and Take Action!

Determine What the Results Tell You

After you stop collecting, summarize your findings in chart, graph, or narrative form, as is appropriate for your results. If you have never analyzed data that includes answers to open-ended questions, you will need to get assistance from someone who has the skills and experience to help you do this. You can also read about analyzing and presenting data in Diamond's *Practical Evaluation Guide* (see "Getting Started Resources").

When you look at the summarized data, you will likely have two responses. The first will be that you have some interesting information that you can use to make some changes. The second will be that you wish you had asked additional or different questions, frequently those that would get at the why of the answers you now have. You will learn a lot about what not to do in your first attempt. Try *not* to feel disheartened or frustrated. You have likely dug up some nuggets of information that you would never have unearthed if you had not made the visitor studies/evaluation leap.

Share Your Findings

Present these nuggets to the board, staff, and volunteers, as well as to your community where appropriate. (Remember those stakeholders we talked about in step 1?) Use the results as a basis for discussion about what the organization might do differently and any questions you still have.

Make Some Real Changes

There is absolutely no point in spending the time to ask these questions if you do not put to good use what you discover. Listen to what your visitors are telling you, and do something differently. (You might consider using the same evaluation after you have made the changes to see if your changes have had the desired effect.) Remember, if you do not use the information you glean from

Table 2.2. Visitor Studies and Evaluation Process

Step 1	Pick a Project
Step 2	Define Desired Outcomes
Step 3	Define the Target Audience
Step 4	Define What You *Need* to Know
Step 5	Review Current Information
Step 6	Choose the Type(s) of Evaluation You Will Do
Step 7	Choose the Methods You Will Use
Step 8	Write Your Questions
Step 9	Collect Data
Step 10	Analyze, Share and Take Action!

your visitor study, there is no point in doing it! And when you make those changes, let your staff, volunteers, members, and visitors know that you made those decisions based on their feedback. Consider a newsletter article about how visitor studies and evaluation changed an exhibit design or programming choice.

Some groups find it helpful to create an evaluation action plan to help clarify what happens next. Table 2.3 provides an example of an evaluation action plan you can use or modify. When you have your first meeting to discuss the results, give everyone a copy of the action plan and discuss the findings, those you will deal with, the changes you will make, the person responsible for making each change, and the deadline for it to be completed.

Visitor studies and evaluation are addictive. Once you realize that useful information is out there, you will be eager to get your hands on it. The challenge is always narrowing your focus and making decisions about your visitor studies and evaluation priorities.

Methods: Pros and Cons

Visitor studies and evaluation methods boil down to variations on two themes: asking people questions (surveys and focus groups) and watching what they do (observations).

Asking Questions

The most common form of visitor studies and evaluation is asking visitors (or nonvisitors) three main types of questions:

- *Close-ended questions* ask the respondent to choose an answer from one or more of a list of choices.
- *Open-ended questions* allow any type of response.
- *Rating questions* ask the respondent to rate the degree to which he or she agrees or disagrees, is satisfied or not satisfied, and so forth.

Table 2.3. Sample Evaluation Action Plan

Finding	Changes Needed*	Person Responsible	Deadline for Completion	Notes
60 percent of respondents complained about lack of parking	No action at this time. No room to expand parking. May consider shuttle buses from nearby site in the future.			
55 percent of respondents want site to be open later	Will plan experiment next summer and keep doors open until 6:30 pm. All PR and website updated to include new hours.	Randy Roberts	Plan for experiment to be completed in four months. Experiment to be conducted in seven months.	Plan should include ways to measure effectiveness of experiment. Will need to recruit more volunteers to keep doors open later.
30 percent of visitors identified the main theme of the exhibit	Will plan an observational/ interview study of the exhibit.	Susan Board	Plan for study to be completed in May. Actual study to be implemented in July.	

* There may be reasons why you might decide to not resolve an issue. It is very important to record that and why you have made that decision so you do not ask questions about this issue in your next survey.

There are also two primary methods for asking questions. If you ask people questions one-on-one, you are using the survey method. If you ask them questions in a group situation in which they listen to and respond to each other, you are conducting a focus group. Because these variations on the theme of question asking have surprisingly different pros and cons, we will look at them separately.

Surveys

Directly asking questions is a great way to obtain demographic information, opinions, and interests and to get at motivation and learning. However, surveys are time intensive in both preparation and analysis. It is challenging to write clear, concise, unambiguous questions, and it usually takes several iterations to come up with a final list. Because surveys can be used to obtain all kinds of desirable information, it can be hard to focus on what you really need. And, in general, surveys tend to produce a positive bias. When you ask somebody a direct question, because we are a polite society, that person will tend to give you a positive answer. Surveys come in their own variations: face-to-face interviews, telephone interviews, and mailed or online questionnaires.

Face-to-face interviews increase interviewees' motivation to answer questions because some very nice person is smiling at them and asking for their time. For that reason, they also are very high in positive bias and more open to subtle (or not so subtle) influence by the interviewer. They are great for open-ended questions because the interviewer's presence tends to motivate the interviewee to give a thoughtful response. The interviewer can also clarify the meaning of the question in response to a confused look from the interviewee (which cannot happen in a written survey). Face-to-face interviews are frequently used within the museum to evaluate the visitor's experience; however, they can be used in other settings to gather information from nonvisitors. Asking people questions about a potential exhibit idea or program outside the grocery store or post office (with permission, of course) is a form of surveying that effectively reaches nonvisitors. Face-to-face interviews use a lot of human resources, as your interviewers may spend a lot of time waiting around for their next interviewee. As stated earlier, the people doing the interviews will need some training on how to invite and motivate interviewees. Tip: When doing face-to-face interviews, wait to ask the demographic questions (e.g., age, race, income) until the end, then hand the clipboard to the visitor and ask him or her to fill out that last section.

Telephone interviews were once quite popular but are fast declining. Research shows that most people would rather do a survey online than on the telephone. If the people you want to reach do not use e-mail or the Internet frequently, such as older, nonvisiting museum members, a telephone interview may be a good choice. Telephone interviews share that ease of question clari-

CASE STUDY: FACE-TO-FACE INTERVIEWS FOR FRONT-END EXHIBIT AND TOUR DEVELOPMENT

Linda Norris,[1] an exhibits developer who has worked as consultant for small museums in the Northeast and in the Ukraine as a Fulbright Scholar, uses face-to-face interviewing to do front-end evaluation in preparation for new exhibits. In just a few minutes, and with a just a few questions related to images, objects, or historical content, she learns what people already know (or do not know) about a topic or means of presentation and what they find interesting. She has frequently been surprised by what the average person does not know about a topic or the misperceptions he or she might have about a time period. Overall, she has found it very helpful in testing assumptions made about visitors.

In preparation for an exhibit about an eighteenth-century site in New York's Hudson Valley, the project team wanted to find out what people knew about 1750. Using a set of index cards listing historical facts, volunteers asked people at a public event (not at the site) to sort the cards into two piles: things that had happened by 1750 and things that had not. Facts on the cards included items such as "New York was a Dutch colony," "Electricity was in use," and "Slavery existed in New York." The team found that most community members knew very little about this era of history. This informed how much basic historical background she needed to provide (a lot!) in the tour development. Without this audience research, she might have created a tour that was accurate and detailed but did not serve as a bridge between visitors' current knowledge and the history of the site.

To help focus an exhibit on the carpet industry, she asked people to sort a set of historic photos into interesting and uninteresting piles. She found that most people were interested in how carpet was made, and fewer people were interested in the people in the images. This information did not mean that she could not tell the stories of the people in the images, but it guided her to include the process of carpet making as a key component of the exhibit. The images she started with were not the most compelling way to share the personal stories of those who worked in the industry.

In one case, she used a single-question survey to help determine what the title of an exhibition should include. The exhibit commemorated a local congressman who was a public figure prominent enough that the post office was named for him. The exhibit committee thought that titling this exhibit with his name was adequate to attract the public. Norris was unsure. So she spent three hours in the very post office named for the congressman asking people putting stamps on their mail who "Mr. John Smith" was. She found that people over forty years old recognized his name immediately, but that those under forty rarely knew anything about him. She could return to the exhibit committee with hard data suggesting that if they wanted younger people to come to the exhibit, they needed a title that explained why a visitor should care about Mr. John Smith.

For another project, she and the exhibit team met with eighth graders to discuss what they liked in an exhibit. Were they interested in computer installations, in labels, in hands-on interactives, in images, in video installations? Every single one of the eighth graders was uninterested in computers in museums. But they were interested in hands-on interactives, in the connection between their local story and larger national issues, and in individual stories.

Norris almost always does some sort of front-end research when working on an exhibit, but she rarely conducts her interviews in the museums that will host them, because she is usually aiming to reach new audiences. So she seeks information where she can reach the general public—outside of grocery stores and public buildings (and always with the permission of property owners). She prefers face-to-face interviews and group conversations to written surveys because she has found that people are rarely motivated to fill out surveys, and she likes being able to follow up with why questions, especially when people have a negative response. Taking the time to gather this information at the beginning of the project has saved her time (and the museums for which she consults' money) as the research helps focus the content of the exhibit or tour early in the process. But she cautions that museums need to be open to the information gained in this kind of research and prepared to adapt their approaches.

Note

1. Linda Norris blogs about her work with museums and history organizations at the Uncataloged Museum at www.uncatalogedmuseum.blogspot.com.

fication with face-to-face interviews. They too are quite expensive in terms of human resource time. Interviewees still show a positive bias (after all, it is still a person on the other end of the phone), but they are less motivated to participate or think hard in comparison with face-to-face interviews. Because this method may be considered annoying, carefully consider whom you are trying to reach before planning a telephone interview.

With *mailed* or *online surveys*, you get the lowest positive bias because respondents can remain anonymous, meaning that you may also receive more honest responses to questions about sensitive topics. Because the questions appear on the page or the screen, this format is good for rankings, checklists, or multiple-choice questions and can also include open-ended questions to determine why respondents rated something high or low or did not like a particular program. It is also useful because visitors have had time to reflect upon their experience at your museum and, as a result, are better able to articulate their opinions. Mailed surveys are probably the most expensive in non–human resources costs, while online surveys are the cheapest in this area. Mailed surveys are also less and less frequently used because of the expense and because of the low response rate. The average rate of response for online surveys is 30–50 percent.

Focus Groups

Asking questions in a group environment is very effective for generating new ideas or brainstorming and for understanding why people feel certain ways about aspects of your museum. Focus groups are frequently used at the beginning of a project to guide big picture thinking with a small group of people who represent the intended audience. They are incredibly helpful in reaching out to both current and new, unfamiliar audiences, and when completed effectively and when their feedback is used, they tend to generate good will. However, leading a focus group and summarizing the information gathered requires a trained and experienced focus group facilitator. For this reason, we highly recommend finding a trained facilitator (perhaps a teacher, businessperson, or professor) to help you with your first focus groups. To find a trained facilitator, contact your field services office, state museum association, or local college or university.

Observation

Watching what people do provides you with a picture of how they actually interact with your activities. Observation can tell you quite a bit about what people are really interested in because they can "vote with their feet." The negative or uninterested feelings come through when you track how little time people spend interacting with your exhibit or engaging in your program.

CASE STUDY: WRITTEN SURVEYS AT THE FOLLETT HOUSE MUSEUM

The Follett House Museum is a branch of the Sandusky Library in Sandusky, Ohio. Maggie Marconi, the full-time museum administrator, had limited experience in visitor studies but was interested to see what she could learn. After mulling over many potential areas, she set the goal of understanding who was coming to the museum and why. A written survey seemed like a manageable project because it wouldn't take staff or volunteer time away from other projects.

Marconi dedicated about forty hours of her time to learning about putting together a written survey, writing and editing it, and entering the data and summarizing the results. (She spent just $23 for clipboards, pencils, and copies.) With the help of the Local History Office of the Ohio Historical Society, she found a nearby expert who guided her in two training sessions. In the first, the expert introduced her to some visitor research theory and then made suggestions on how to write good survey questions and provided some examples. At the second session, the expert reviewed her draft questions, helped her pick out the most useful questions, and fine-tuned the wording, as well as set up an Excel spreadsheet to analyze the survey responses. Marconi found that avoiding leading language in the questions was one of the most challenging aspects of the process.

Over one summer, Follett House Museum docents asked every visitor to participate in the optional five-minute survey before their visit, and they collected 196 responses. The ten-question survey focused on why the visitor decided to visit, how the visitor learned about the museum, what his or her expectations for the visit were, and demographic information.

Marconi learned that the typical Follett House Museum visitor was a Caucasian woman, over sixty, who came for the first time with a group of friends. That visitor usually found out about the museum by word of mouth and visited because she wanted to learn something new. Marconi was surprised to find out how many visitors just dropped in on a whim, and this led her to think about ways that she could enhance the profile of the museum so that more people were more aware of it as a place to spend an afternoon.

In the two years since collecting the data, Marconi has worked more closely with other museums in the Sandusky area to cross-promote each other and build on the successful word-of-mouth publicity. She has looked

(*continued*)

at advertising opportunities more carefully and participated in the Ohio Department of Transportation brochure distribution system. And she has worked each year to create new temporary signage to catch the eye of people walking or driving by, including yard signs and a vinyl banner for an annual countywide cooperative museum event.

Although Marconi noted that she still has more to learn from the survey data and that the process has prompted a lot of reflection about her audience, she is ready to begin gathering data again. She plans to use the same survey to gauge how effective her advertising and cross-promotion efforts have been, as well as to ask questions of the separate audience she serves with her local history programs offered at the library.

The most important thing to investigate is why people are doing what they are doing in an exhibit or tour. To determine this, you need to follow up each observation with a brief interview with visitors you are watching so that you can find out why they did what they did. Some of the questions you might want to ask after observing someone in an exhibit or tour might be "Were any objects memorable for you, and if so, why were they memorable?" or "What do you think the main point of this exhibit is?"

No Silver Bullets

No matter how long you have been working in a small museum, you know that there are no silver bullets. Most of the things you want to do take longer than expected and are interrupted by minor emergencies, helpful volunteers, and those pesky but all-important visitors. You need to make good decisions about how you eke out the most from your valuable human resources and limited funds. You need to demonstrate your value to your community. And you want to create more engaging exhibits, to host programs that attract a wide variety of people, and to be the place where everyone in your community feels welcome, respected, and comfortable. You need and want these things, even when you are exhausted from your juggling act. So start today. Pick one thing that you would like to know from your audience. Order one of the resources below through interlibrary loan. Learn how to do valid and reliable visitor studies. Talk about it with your colleagues. We strongly recommend that you collaborate with other historic sites or nonprofit cultural organizations in your community to do some

Photo 2.1. As a result of visitor surveys conducted by the Follett House Museum in Sandusky, Ohio, the staff decided that temporary signage would help attract and remind potential drop-in visitors of the museum's offerings. Future surveys will help them determine if their strategy was successful. (Courtesy of the Follett House Museum, a branch of the Sandusky Library)

CASE STUDY: FOCUS GROUPS AT THE HOWARD COUNTY HISTORICAL SOCIETY

In Kokomo, Indiana, a county historical society uses focus groups to gather information about collecting priorities. The Howard County Historical Society (HCHS) developed the following mission statement to guide its efforts: "The Howard County Historical Society believes in the daily relevance of history. As the custodian of Howard County's unique heritage, the society preserves our community's collective experiences. In sharing that history, we foster a sense of community—connecting us to our neighbors, the past to the future, and our home to the world."

When Delphi—an international business with its headquarters in Howard County—offered HCHS seven filing cabinets' worth of materials, along with a few three-dimensional pieces, curators Stew Lauterbach and Bonnie Van Kley were not sure what they wanted to keep. A few years before this donation, the staff developed themes to guide their collecting and exhibition plans, with the contributions from several focus groups within the community. In that process, they determined that local industry, including the stories and collections of Delco Radio/Delphi, is a major theme, so they knew they wanted to keep some portion of the material—but how were they to decide what to keep? Instead of making a decision in a vacuum, the curators chose again to seek community input.

With the short-term goal of making decisions about the donation and the long-term goal of narrowing down the most important topics and stories of Delco Radio/Delphi, they invited fifteen to twenty people representing executives, engineers, and labor union leaders to participate in a series of focus groups. A retired Delco Radio/Delphi focus group manager volunteered to lead the meetings. After three meetings, the staff had enough direction to make good decisions about the donation; they refused slides about an aerospace project because most of that work was done in another state, while they accepted a tie tack depicting a helmet radio because it was manufactured in Howard County and used in Vietnam. This tie tack has the staff actively seeking a helmet radio, which is much more significant to the collection.

As of this writing, the group has not whittled down its stories and themes to a manageable number yet, but it has helped the staff set some parameters related to the time period they will collect. The staff believes that some of the delay is because it is very difficult to reach a consensus about what stories can be eliminated with a group that is so close to the story. In addition, the loss of their skilled facilitator after the third meeting (because he took a job in another state) hindered the process. While focus groups can provide a wealth of information, a leader who can keep the group on task is a must. However, the focus group members have also become invested in the museum, seeing it as a place where their story will be told and where they can meet with past colleagues.

The HCHS staff has not yet reached its goal of ten or fewer Delco stories on which to focus their collections efforts, but because of their focus groups, they are on the path toward a much more proactive and community-informed collecting effort.

evaluation. And become the museum that is always improving, always better meeting the needs of its audience, so that one day your visitors will wonder just how it was that you read their minds.

Resources

Many resources are available to you related to audience research, visitor studies, and evaluation. We encourage you to join the Visitors' Voices affinity group of the American Association for State and Local History (AASLH) to have access to experts and other small museum paid and unpaid staff who are working on visitor studies and evaluation and who might recommend new or targeted resources for your particular project. To join, go to www.aaslh.org/visitors-voices. You do not have to be a member of AASLH to join this affinity group. You might also want to contact a field services office in your state or region to get advice or information about local resources and experts or your state museum association. Visit www.aaslh.org/FSA/FSA.html to locate your field services representatives. (Not all states have a field services office. If you are in one of those states, consider contacting a regional group or a nearby state's office to get started.)

CASE STUDY: OBSERVATION AT THE NETTLE CREEK VALLEY MUSEUM

With the goal of improving exhibits in mind, Jeff Harris, director of the Nettle Creek Valley Museum in Hagerstown, Indiana, decided to map where visitors spent their time. The museum space is one large room, visible from the docent post at the front door. Harris created a tally sheet that listed the fifteen topical exhibits scattered throughout the room. For a few weeks, Harris asked his docents to put a hash mark next to each exhibit a visitor stopped to look at. It did not matter how long visitors viewed a display or what they did while stopped, so the system was simple and easy to use for the docents—all of whom knew the exhibits well. The docents were able to track almost every visitor, as people usually came alone or in groups of two or three.

Harris discovered that some exhibits were surprisingly popular, such as the display on a local business responsible for the creation of cruise control for automobiles. Other exhibits that he had assumed would be of interest, such as a display on the early efforts to build a canal through the town, garnered few tally marks. Looking at the overall pattern, he found that people stopped most at exhibits that shared stories unique to the area and were less packed with artifacts.

Although he did not know exactly why visitors stopped where they did (and he could have if the observations had been followed with a few questions), Harris used the information to make changes in the exhibits. For example, he created a new display about the canals—using far fewer documents and artifacts and creating a more immersive experience by building a small canal boat dock. When docents repeated the observation system again, the canal exhibit was much more popular. Harris used the hard data showing the increase in stops to advocate with his board to devote more resources to improving exhibits and to demonstrate that "less is more."

OBSERVING A TOUR IN A HISTORIC HOUSE

Conny Graft finds that conducting observations of visitors while they are on a tour can not only reveal helpful insights about visitor behavior but also assist interpreters (or tour guides or docents) in understanding how their behavior impacts visitors.

Graft begins by determining what behavioral outcomes the staff wants visitors to exhibit during the tour. For example, if you decide that you want the tour to be conversational, then you would have an outcome that says, "During the tour visitors will be encouraged to share their stories about some of the objects on the tour," or "During the tour visitors will be able to look at the objects in the room and tell the interpreter which objects are most interesting to them and why." Not only is articulating the behaviors you want visitors to exhibit during the tour a necessary step for conducting observations, but it is also a key step in helping interpreters understand how you want them to share the history of your site with visitors.

The next step is to go on several tours and jot down on a small notepad some of the behaviors visitors exhibit during the tour. Then turn the behaviors into codes—for instance, "looking at their watch" can be written down as "watch" or "talking to each other" can be "talk/other" versus "talk/guide," which would indicate talking with the guide.

Create an observation sheet with the list of behaviors in one column with space next to each where you can mark down each time you observe the behavior. (Excel or another spreadsheet program is a good tool for doing this.) Also leave some empty space to jot down behaviors that are not on your list. Share the observation sheet with your interpreters so they know what you are looking for and how you will be doing the observation.

As a side note, Graft also recommends training interpreters to conduct the observations so they can see the tour from the other side of the fence. When doing this at a site, after a fairly new interpreter completed her first observation and survey, she came running up and said, "Conny, it's just not true what they say in the break room!" She then went on to explain that in the break room, interpreters told her that most visitors do not listen to a thing you say, so do not worry about what you say. Then the new interpreter revealed that she had followed a young father with a fussy baby on the tour, and she was sure that he had not been listening and was not interested in history. To her surprise, the young man was a big history fan and remembered

(continued)

TEXTBOX 2.11 (*Continued*)

almost everything about the tour, and they had a great conversation discussing some of the topics he had just heard about.

Using random sample selection (the first, second, or third visitor to walk past a specific landmark), choose one visitor to observe. While it may be hard to believe, Graft has rarely had visitors ask her what she is writing down when she is doing observations—they are too interested in either the interpreter or what is in the room they are entering. When asked, she replies, "I am evaluating the tours today," and usually that is enough explanation. At the end of the tour, as the visitor she is observing exits the tour, she approaches him or her and conducts a brief survey.

Observations should always be followed up by a survey. Understanding behaviors is tricky. Graft has had several experiences where she has observed a visitor smiling, nodding his head up and down, and even clapping at the end of the tour acting as if happy with it; then, during the interview, she has discovered that the visitor was just being polite and was actually bored or not happy with the tour. The questions on the follow-up survey need to solicit feedback about the content of the tour, how it was delivered, what one thing the visitor took away from the tour, and suggestions for improvement.

When reporting on the findings, count up the number of behaviors you observed that met your behavioral outcomes and those you saw that did not. Share the observations and survey results with the staff, and determine whether you need to make changes based on the results. Make the changes and repeat the observation to see if you were able to improve your ability to meet your outcomes.

Below you will find a list of resources to get you started on your project, as well as other resources that may help you dig deeper into various aspects of visitor studies and evaluation.

Getting Started Resources

Diamond, Judy. *Practical Evaluation Guide: Tools for Museums and Other Informal Educational Settings.* 2nd ed. Lanham, MD: AltaMira Press, 2009.

Graft, Conny. "Listen, Evaluate, Respond!" *History News* 62, no. 2 (spring 2007): 12–16.

Korn, Randi. "Studying Your Visitors: Where to Begin." *History News* 49, no. 2 (March–April 1994): 23–26.

Lewis, Andrea. "Surveying Visitors, Plain and Simple." *History News* 62, no 2 (spring 2007): 17–19.

Shaping Outcomes (www.shapingoutcomes.org): Developed through a cooperative agreement between the Institute of Museum and Library Services and Indiana University–Purdue University Indianapolis, with faculty from the Museum Studies Program and English Department of the Indiana University School of Liberal Arts and School of Library and Information Science.

Sharken Simon, Judith. *The Wilder Nonprofit Field Guide to Conducting Successful Focus Groups.* St. Paul, MN: Amherst H. Wilder Foundation, 1999.

Visitor Research Databases

Informal Science (www.informalscience.org): This is the best database of evaluation and research reports for visitor behavior in museums, zoos, parks, botanical gardens, and science museums. Some of the best studies have been conducted in science museums, and you can use those studies to inform the decisions you make about how to do evaluation in history museums. On the home page, type what you are looking for into the search box. Examples of search terms include the following: "history museums," "history exhibits," "studies on orientation," "field trip studies," "teacher studies," and "website studies," among others.

Exploratorium Visitor Research and Evaluation (www.exploratorium.edu/partner/visitor_research/reports.php): Search by study type or keyword.

Office of Policy and Analysis at the Smithsonian Institution (www.si.edu/opanda/studies_of_visitors.html): This website includes copies of all visitor studies conducted at the Smithsonian.

Harper's Ferry Center Media Evaluation and Visitor Studies (www.nps.gov/hfc/products/evaluate.htm): This is the evaluation center for the National Park Service, and this website includes all the visitor studies conducted in national parks across the country.

Other Helpful Resources

American Association of Museums: Committee on Audience Research and Evaluation (www.care-aam.org): Members of AAM can join this standing professional committee to access a network of professional researchers who focus just on museums.

Museum Audience Insight (www.reachadvisors.typepad.com/museum_audience_insight): This blog and newsletter provides ongoing information about nationwide studies of users of U.S. museums and libraries.

Randi Korn & Associates (www.randikorn.com): Randi Korn is an evaluator and has made available many useful articles, presentations, and case studies in the resources section of her website.

Stein, Jill, Marianna Adams, and Jessica Luke. "Thinking Evaluatively: A Practical Guide to Integrating the Visitor Voice," AASLH Technical Leaflet 238, *History News* 62, no. 2 (spring 2007).

Visitor Studies Association (www.visitorstudies.org): This is a great resource for workshops, training, publications, and links to other resources, as well as for networking with people who do visitor studies for a living.

Notes

1. Thanks to Jeff Harris for the title and case studies and for supporting Stacy Klingler in pursuing this project. Thanks to all the staffs of small and medium-sized museums who shared real-world stories about their efforts to do good research and evaluation, even if their examples did not make it into this chapter: Lindsey Baker, Sarah Clark, Anne Guernsey, Dale Jones, Kelly Karickhoff, Stew Lauterbach, Maggie Marconi, Linda Norris, Lisa Simmons, George Squibb, Sonja Thune, Bonnie Van Kley, and Amanda Burke Wesselmann.

2. To find data for your state and then your county or city/town, go to http://quickfacts .census.gov/qfd/index.html. Choose your state to get data for your entire state. Within your state page, you can limit your search by county or city. On either the state page or the city/county page, you will see in the right-hand corner of the page "Want More? Browse data sets for . . ." Clicking on this link allows you to choose different kinds of information, including "General Demographic Characteristics" for the sex, age, and race categories applicable for your area. To find 2010 data for your state, go to www.factfinder2.census.gov and watch the video on how to find data for your area. You can also sign up for the Census Bureau blog to find out when your state will be added to the website.

CHAPTER THREE
LIKE A GOOD NEIGHBOR: COMMUNITY ADVOCACY FOR SMALL MUSEUMS

Barbara B. Walden

Community Service Is Essential to Any Small Museum

As the world around us expands and technology improves our communication methods and abilities, the opportunity for small museums to engage their neighbors and take a more active role in their local communities has never been greater. Community service is at the heart of museum identity and mission; likewise our local communities are devoted to helping one another and enriching people's lives at a local level. Both museums and civic leadership are dedicated to building a sense of identity and strengthening community connections. They differ only in their focus: History museums focus on the past, while civic leadership attempts to improve the present. Within our multifaceted existence as historians, collections managers, storytellers, and administrators, we must always turn to the needs of our local constituents when creating and strengthening our role within the community. As museums begin to advocate for their neighbors, they soon discover the museum mission and the community mission are one and the same. Museums that invest locally, whether through community service, education, or leadership, are also pleased to discover their return in the form of museum loyalty, volunteer service, and support.

Becoming a strong advocate within the local community is not just about promoting your small museum or historic site as an engaging venue; it is about connecting the community and site in order to provide insight and inspiration to those who are seeking an experience that transcends the ordinary. In order to achieve this, small museums have to identify what is distinct and unique about their shared story and, while continuing to preserve their community's collective narrative, create an environment that encourages and supports dialogue. Small museums need to recognize that the story of place is just as much about a community's future as it is about its shared past. Local residents may not be able to recite your site's mission by memory, list the details of the prized pieces in the collection, or remember the date on which the historic home was built, but they will be able to recognize that your small museum is essential to maintaining or improving the vibrancy of life in the community.

This chapter primarily examines the community advocacy approach of the Kirtland Temple, a small historic site located in Kirtland, Ohio. Like many small museums, the Kirtland Temple has very few resources to spend on publicity and promotions or the luxury of a sizeable staff to pursue extensive outreach, community relations, or marketing endeavors. This site is used as a case study to reveal how the National Historic Landmark served this local community beyond its historical property. The experiences of other historic sites across the country serve as examples of simple approaches that small museums can take in cultivating support and awareness within their communities.

Center of Community Life: Kirtland Temple

Over the past two decades, the members of Kirtland Temple staff have demonstrated how a small museum, limited in staff and resources, can accomplish incredible community relationships and support. Although their actions responded to a unique crisis, the steps the Kirtland Temple staff took can easily be replicated in any small museum's attempt to improve community relations: opening dialogue with the museum's neighbors, taking an active role in local civic organizations, and offering museum resources to meet community needs.

Towering over the northeastern Ohio hills, the Kirtland Temple stands as a vivid reminder that Kirtland was once home to one of the largest nineteenth-century utopian communities in U.S. history.[1] The historic house of worship was the first temple built by the followers of Joseph Smith. As the temple builders laid the rough stone walls, they dreamed the temple would become the "center of community life" as a place for education, administration, and worship for the Kirtland community. At the height of the Latter-Day Saint community in 1838, nearly two thousand members of the Mormon faith lived in Kirtland. By the following year, only one hundred Mormons remained. Today, volunteer interpreters share a compelling a story as they accompany visitors through a remarkable three-story historic house of worship. Unique architectural elements include two large assembly rooms located on the first and second floors, nine tiered pulpits at both ends of the sanctuary and second-floor classroom, choir lofts in all four corners of the sanctuary, and pew boxes with moveable benches that allow visitors to face either end of the two large assembly rooms. Designated a National Historic Landmark in 1977 for its religious and architectural significance, the small historic site hosts tens of thousands of visitors from all over the world.

The Kirtland Temple complex consists of a visitor center, five acres of lawns and gardens, and an outdoor gathering space. The site's budget is meager but allows for three full-time staff members (a director and two-person maintenance

Photo 3.1. Kirtland Temple, located in Kirtland, Ohio. (Courtesy of Barbara Walden)

crew) and a part-time bookkeeper. Volunteers form the backbone of the historic site and play a significant role in preserving, interpreting, and maintaining the temple and visitor center.

The community of Kirtland, Ohio, prides itself as the "City of Faith and Beauty." Located twenty-two miles east of Cleveland, Kirtland is a bedroom community with seventy-five hundred residents scattered across seventeen square miles. The city is home to a small library, a civic center, and one K–12 public school system. Parks, educational facilities, public institutions, and churches own 30 percent of Kirtland's total acreage.

For several decades the Kirtland Temple had maintained a fairly quiet existence, serving a tourist population that traveled through each summer while largely ignoring, or not initiating relationships with, the local community. Site personnel were often so consumed with the responsibilities of maintaining the site that they did not have the time or resources to devote to cultivating community relations. Kirtland residents rarely considered the historic site in their daily lives, except when family or friends visited from out of town. As is the case with most local historical resources, the locals had a "been there, done that" attitude to the site. In the eyes of the community, the temple was not a part of its history but rather a cultural remnant of a unique religious group that had moved in and out almost two hundred years earlier. Kirtlanders did not see the temple as part of their historical identity; therefore, it was nonexistent in their daily routine. However, the Kirtland community's apathy toward the historic site changed drastically in 1989.

In the late 1980s, Kirtland experienced a significant tragedy that left a lasting mark. In the winter of 1989, sheriff's deputies, responding to an anonymous tip, discovered the bodies of Dennis and Sheryl Avery, along with their three young daughters, buried in a barn located on a Kirtland farm. The parents of the deceased family were once followers of Jeffrey Donald Lundgren, a charismatic cult leader who had resided in the farmhouse located only steps away from the barn and burial site. Immediately after the Avery bodies were discovered, a nationwide manhunt ensued. Authorities located members of the Lundgren cult, including Jeff Lundgren, and all were brought to trial for the Avery family murders.[2] As Lundgren considered himself a living prophet of the Mormon faith, the media frequently used the Kirtland Temple as a backdrop as the story of the Lundgren murders unfolded in the national spotlight. The sensationalized court hearings and the national media frenzy portrayed Kirtland as a small town that housed cults and encouraged their behavior, while the Kirtland Temple was frequently used as an irrational symbol for what happens when religious cults go too far. Almost immediately, community members had two strong emotional reactions to the tragic event: (1) concern for the safety of their families, and (2) defensiveness about how their community was being portrayed to the nation through the media. The apathy once felt for the Kirtland Temple was soon replaced by highly charged negative views of the historic site. It was a public relations nightmare.

Realizing the immediate need for community action to counter growing public anger and suspicion, Kirtland's religious and civic leaders held a meeting to discuss the city's response to the Avery family murders. This coalition, including staff from the Kirtland Temple, agreed that Kirtland's civic and religious leaders needed to communicate with the larger community. Out of a series of gatherings, these leaders created the Kirtland Ministerial Alliance with the intention of strengthening the lines of communication between church and civic leadership. The goals of the alliance were to (1) increase awareness of Kirtland's niche religious and civic communities, (2) open dialogue between leaders so that community concerns could be addressed, and (3) schedule a regular meeting where such concerns could be aired and awareness improved.

The Kirtland Temple staff's involvement in the Kirtland Ministerial Alliance helped community leaders recognize that various media outlets were attaching a stigma to the historic site as a symbol of the Kirtland community. The alliance immediately began planning for a community-wide gathering in the form of a worship service. The gathering was intended to give residents an

Photo 3.2. Annual Community Service: The annual service, held in the Kirtland Temple, began over twenty years ago as a compassionate response to a community tragedy and is led by the city's civic and religious leaders. (Courtesy of Barbara Walden)

emotional and spiritual outlet, to demystify beliefs and counter false assumptions about any single religious group in the community, and to strengthen residents' identification with Kirtland over any subgroup affiliation, religious or otherwise. The worship service was held in the sanctuary of the Kirtland Temple, a location chosen because of its indirect connection to the murders and because of the ensuing controversy. Kirtland's leadership recognized the potential to turn the now stigmatized temple into a community symbol of strength and unity.

Over the next two decades, staff at the Kirtland Temple built a strong relationship with the Kirtland community. Once a symbol of a tragic event in Kirtland's history, the Kirtland Temple is now perceived by local residents as a treasured historic icon and place for open dialogue. This change did not come easily for staff at the Kirtland Temple. Two site directors and several volunteers worked tirelessly to improve community relations on a minimal budget. A number of lessons were learned in the journey toward creating and strengthening community advocacy.

Community Relationships and Service

Although the Kirtland Temple example is a unique community relations experience for a small museum, the response of the temple staff in cultivating relationships and trust within the local community is not. The approach the staff took to improving community relations is easily adapted to other small museums. The process of creating relationships within the municipality with the intended outcome of cultivating strong community advocacy is one of giving and receiving with neighbors as equals. This may be the most difficult step for museum leaders pursuing an advocacy role within the community. Small museum staff and board members must approach their communities with a fresh perspective, attempting to understand how the organization with limited resources (staff, budget, space, etc.) can serve the needs of the community first and foremost. Out of the relationships created, small museum professionals and community leaders will discover new and exciting ways that both parties can benefit through collaboration. It is important that small museum staffs and boards recognize that community service and advocacy are much larger and more important than the small museum alone.

Following the tragedy, the Kirtland Temple staff recognized that the community's once apathetic perception of the site resulted from the insignificant role the site played within the community. Staff members rarely ventured outside the historic property to engage the community. The community perceived the site and its history as irrelevant to their lives, and the small museum exhibited similar feelings toward the community. Local residents were not large donors, rarely visited the site, and, as a result, were irrelevant to the site personnel. However, the staff's perception of the community and the museum's inactive involvement on the local level changed dramatically following the tragedy. Staff members became involved in the local Kiwanis chapter and helped raise funds for the construction of a new public library—one temple volunteer sat on the fundraising committee for the new library, while another acted as the Kiwanis president, and a third sat on the Kiwanis board of directors. Although there was no immediate benefit to the site, having staff connect with the community in such a way personalized the site. Within a few years, opportunities would arise within the Kirtland area, and site personnel would be contacted with requests from a broad spectrum of local residents. High-caliber individuals, from city officials and county politicians to the neighbor down the street, began requesting special tours for their guests and recommending site personnel to give brown-bag lectures for their community groups.

Small museums across the country are discovering additional low-cost approaches to heightening their role within the local community. Site directors and museum curators are approaching school districts to explore career development programs with special-needs students. Museum store projects are excellent exercises for special-needs teachers searching for skills development opportunities in real work environments for students. In addition, high school career counselors often seek local businesses and nonprofits where students can earn community service hours. While their skill levels and maturity vary, students are quite capable of assisting with landscaping historical gardens, filling customer service positions, serving as administrative assistants, developing educational programs and traveling trunks, and leading interpretive programs. The experience in a small museum not only benefits students with a line on their resumes but, more importantly, also helps build their self-confidence before they jump into the workforce. Small museums must take advantage of this opportunity to invest in the community's youth as potential lifelong supporters of the small museum.

An additional angle a small museum may wish to consider is the role of its site in the local economy. In 2005, the staff at the Kirtland Temple made the painful decision to begin charging a $2 admission fee for tours—the museum and gardens remained free. Each visitor touring the temple received a small sticker to wear that stated, "I'm helping to preserve the Kirtland Temple." Following the temple tour, visitors would often forget that they were wearing the stickers as they wandered into local restaurants, stores, gas stations, and the like. This simple stickered statement communicated to the local businesses the financial impact the historic site had on the local economy. Within two months, the staff at the Kirtland Temple had received invitations to dine at—and recommend— local restaurants. A number of business owners dropped off informational flyers for site visitor interest. A small admission fee evolved into a financial statement about the increasing role of the small museum within the local economy.

Model Leadership within Your Community: Become the Eyes and Ears of the Your Neighborhood

Although not every community has an alliance of civic and religious leaders, small museum leaders do have the ability to take an active role in local organizations such as the Rotary Club, Kiwanis International, the chamber of commerce, and the city or county visitors' bureau. Most community organizations have minimal requirements for members outside of a weekly meeting and annual dues. However, small museum leaders need to take advantage of such organizations as an opportunity to hear local voices and gain a better understanding of community needs in order to know how the museum can better position itself within the region. These organizations are actively searching for new members and fresh ideas.

Membership in community organizations not only provides a unique opportunity for small museum board and staff members to serve the needs of local residents but can also be an excellent source of community advocacy and site promotions. Kiwanis International, for example, has 260,000 adult members in eight thousand clubs in over ninety countries across the world; it also includes a number of youth affiliates, such as Circle K (college and university), Key Club (high school), Builders Club (middle school), and K-Kids (elementary school). By becoming an advisor for any one of the Kiwanis affiliates, the small museum leader makes an immediate connection with the local schools. The community leadership position is automatically accompanied by the opportunity to see firsthand the outside impression of your museum and the relevance of your site within the community.

Discovering a leadership opportunity or role for the community at your museum is just as crucial as becoming an active face in the community. As small museum leaders become familiar with local organizations, boards, and services, they will have a stronger understanding of how their museum's mission fits into the needs of the community. In their article "A Golden Age for Historic Properties," John Durel and Anita Nowery Durel propose that more museums need to take advantage of group interests within the community by creating a variety of affinity groups. Examples include gardeners' guilds, history researchers, antique enthusiasts, musicians, and so forth. The authors suggest that the museum not confine the opportunities of such groups or limit their freedoms but embrace "whatever any group of individuals might want that makes legitimate use of the organization's resources. Each affinity group would plan and implement its own programs and activities for its own members as well as others."[3] This is not an entirely new concept, as most small museums and historic sites are familiar with volunteers who hold a variety of responsibilities at the site, including landscaping, collections care, visitor service, interpretation, and research. However, John Durel and Anita Nowery Durel's approach invites the small museum to let go of its traditional management style and allow the community more access to the site, to move from its traditional role as history interpreter to become an experience facilitator.

In 2009, the Kirtland Temple staff attempted a new approach as facilitators in collaboration with the local community's middle school students. Since a member of the temple staff was an active advisor to the Kiwanis Builders Club, middle school students were chosen from the club membership and invited to create an exhibit titled "Calling Kirtland Home." A select number of students were invited to take ten photographs of what they considered special about their home community. They included photographs of the high school football field, their individual houses, the Kirtland library, a local tavern, and a friendly neighborhood cat. The students were then asked to select three photographs that expressed what they found most profound about Kirtland and to include a written paragraph on each image explaining why it described this special characteristic of their community. The images and narrative were to be exhibited at the Kirtland visitor center as an opportunity for visitors to learn about the local community from the unique perspective of Kirtland's middle school students. The project naturally made the middle school students take an active role in the interpretation of their community, as well as gave them a sense of personal ownership in how the community was portrayed to out-of-state visitors.

Discovering a Need within Your Community

Every museum leader has an innate sense that museums and historic sites are essential. However, the challenge arrives in convincing those who are not avid history enthusiasts of this truth. Museum staff and board members must look to the museum's neighbors to find the intersection of museum and community needs. For example, museums and historic sites across the country open their doors on Election Day to host local voters as a designated polling place. This simple action meets the needs of the local community (by providing a place to vote), while also meeting the needs of the small museum (by generating community awareness, publicity, and promotions). It is important for small museums to expand their services outside their general mission as a place for interpreting and preserving local history. This expansion is not limited to involvement in other community-minded organizations but includes extending the mission of the site to include community service. Small museums and historic sites must learn to stretch their missions to include the interpretation of the universality of the human experience and also to raise the importance of the distinct and unique qualities of the place and the people connected with the shared local story.

The Kirtland experience is an example of how a small historic site used a local tragedy and a public relations fiasco to unite a community with an annual event and monthly leadership gatherings at minimal cost. The temple staff, consisting primarily of volunteers, saw a need within the community for a place of solace and compassion during a time of tragedy. Through the site's involvement in the Kirtland Ministerial Alliance, it was chosen as a logical, if controversial, location for an important community gathering. Importantly, however, the site continued building community relationships outside the first worship service. With the collaboration of the alliance, the one-time event became an annual tradition. The site director facilitates the event and involves participants from the schools, police department, fire department, and all nine churches. It is a Rockwellian experience. The temple also takes an active role in organizing the monthly meetings at which the alliance continues improving communication among Kirtland's leadership.

A small house museum in Lamoni, Iowa, discovered a unique approach to community advocacy and service that stretched outside the daily responsibilities of the site.[4] Known locally as historic Liberty Hall, this nineteenth-century house museum is volunteer managed and maintained. Site director Martha McKain plays an active role in her community by hosting special events, conducting education programs, and partnering with the schools. In the spring of

2004, Liberty Hall's volunteers began to stretch their tradition of community outreach further. In collaboration with a community organization, they advocated for a bicycle trail that explored Lamoni from the east to the west through various landscapes and ended at the steps of Liberty Hall's front porch. With the assistance of several organizations, the bicycle trail became a reality for community residents. Liberty Hall staff perceived their new community role as one of warm hospitality for their neighbors. New tables and benches were built and installed for weary bikers. Continuing with educational goals, new interpretive signage was installed to educate the bikers about the history of Liberty Hall.[5]

Drayton Hall, a historic plantation located on the banks of the Ashley River in South Carolina, is an excellent example of how a historic site can play a leading role in advocating for the needs of the local community. Although the site is not considered a small museum, Drayton Hall's experience in the Ashley River region is a model example of community advocacy. The staff at this historic home has been involved in regional preservation for decades; however, a significant need for conservation arose in 2004 when a developer threatened to turn sixty-five hundred acres of woodlands into suburban track housing, a commercial center, a golf course, and a hotel. The site was located a few miles from Drayton Hall, and the potential development would drastically alter the historic landscape and culture of the river region with the construction of a four-lane expressway through the once serene neighborhood. If this was allowed to occur, further development along the Ashley River was certain. As one can only imagine, community members were alarmed. The staff at Drayton Hall did not ignore the concerns of their neighbors—quite the contrary. They became actively involved in challenging the intentions of the out-of-state developers. George W. McDaniel, Drayton Hall's executive director, explained, "To challenge this development, Drayton Hall engaged the community by partnering with nearby historic sites, neighborhood associations, as well as individual residents, local political leaders, conservation and preservation organizations, and taxpayer associations. We also involved the community through the print and broadcast media and through public hearings and rallies."[6] McDaniel and his staff recognized that they could not challenge the powerful developers alone, as the site and staff simply did not have the resources to win. Using community collaborations and the assistance of the South Carolina Coastal Conservation League, the University of South Carolina, and the National Trust for Historic Preservation's legal department, the historic site persevered and managed to prevent a catastrophe for the life and culture of the Ashley River region. It also benefitted from the campaign by forging relationships with new audiences, discovering previously unknown sources of support, and enhancing the site's profile within the community. McDaniel reflected, "In contemplating this experience, several factors were key for us to engage our community. First, we had a strategic plan articulating

Photo 3.3.   Walking path in Lamoni, Iowa. (Courtesy of Barbara Walden)

our vision, our mission, and our goals, of which regional preservation was one. Second, we took a leadership role, but also followed, and we partnered with a range of allies. And finally, we had the strong support of our board, staff, and membership to sustain the organization for the long haul (and fortunately, the funding—all of which are interrelated)."[7]

Role of Community Education and Your Institution

Opportunities abound in every community to collaborate with local schools, museums, and learning facilities in the development of education programs, from distance learning to science investigation in the gardens. The secret to collaboration is simply becoming involved in the world outside of the museum walls. As staff members venture out into the local community, they must do so with the willingness to be genuine, flexible, and patient. Being disingenuous and superficial in community relations will do more damage to the small museum than if the representative had simply stayed at home and continued ignoring the local community.

Small museums must be open to the needs of their neighbors, even when it means providing a service to the local community that involves a new interpretation of their mission.

The staff at the Kirtland Temple reached beyond the site's history focus to meet a growing curricular need for tangible local math examples. As an active advisor for the local Key Club at the Kirtland High School, the site director was approached by the high school art teacher with an invitation to collaborate on a distance-learning program with the Cleveland Museum of Art. The high school teacher happened to be a volunteer educator at the art museum and was approached by its education director, who was looking for significant historic sites that were willing to collaborate on a project that fulfilled Ohio's academic curriculum standards. The art teacher immediately thought of the Kirtland Temple as he had observed the staff's involvement in the local community. With the help of a local high school math teacher and the staff at the Cleveland Museum of Art, a distance-learning program titled "Sacred Landmarks" was created. The temple was used as an architectural example of several math equations. The simple step away from a history focus into the realm of mathematics was a challenging stretch for the staff. However, the benefits of collaborating with the Cleveland Museum of Art and the Kirtland High School opened the door for future partnerships.

Educational collaborations are nothing new to the staff at Liberty Hall in Lamoni, Iowa. The small town's struggling economy is sustained by Graceland University, a private college located within Lamoni's city limits. Shortly after learning of the needs of the struggling history department, Liberty Hall began offering a number of internship opportunities for students interested in a hands-on experience in the history field. A field trip to Liberty Hall is now included on the syllabus for the undergraduate class "Historical Inquiry," a core requirement for all students seeking a bachelor's in history at Graceland. However, Martha McKain and her staff also meet Graceland's needs outside of the history department. In 2009, the historic site partnered with the international studies program

Photo 3.4. Joseph Smith III's Liberty Hall, a small house museum in Lamoni, Iowa, is an excellent example of a small museum identifying the needs of its unique community and lending both leadership and site support toward meeting those needs. (Courtesy of Barbara Walden)

in offering a volunteer opportunity to a student from Russia who was studying at Graceland University.

Embrace Community Involvement in Museum Interpretation, Education, and Exhibits

The process of creating a museum environment in which members of the community feel both invested and comfortable may be a challenge for some. Small museums have the ability to become a venue for hosting discussion groups and classes, all the while becoming a premier site in the community for civic leaders and local pride. Do not be afraid to explore the role of the small museum in incorporating the community in exhibit design, unique interpretive programs, website involvement, and commemorative events.

In 2005, the staff at the Kirtland Temple launched a fundraising campaign for a new visitor center. The existing two-thousand-square-foot visitor center contained only nine hundred square feet of public space. Although community outreach services were improving the relationship with the community, the World War II–era visitor center was inadequate in terms of space and poorly maintained. As the staff began to write exhibit labels and select artifacts for the new museum exhibition space, they posed the question, "What does the Kirtland resident want to experience in exhibits?" With relationships already created through various community organizations, it was fairly easy to gather the local civic and religious leaders, along with a number of prominent residents, together for an afternoon summit at the library. What began as a simple gathering to talk about prospective history topics for the museum exhibits turned into a stimulating discussion about what the community desired to see throughout the historic property, including interpretive programs and garden landscapes; also raised were maintenance concerns, the desire for community events, and a need for a community gathering place. No longer were the museum exhibits the topic of discussion. School administrators commented on how the gardens could be expanded, local ministers inquired about spiritual formation programming and the need for a labyrinth within the community (the temple's gardens being a prime geographic location), the local librarian inquired about a research library, and the Kiwanis president asked about banquet options in the new theater. By the end of the afternoon, several additional meetings were planned, and on-site tours were promised.

Two years later, the staff at the Kirtland Temple hosted the grand opening of a brand new visitor center. The Kirtland mayor delivered a speech at the opening event, and several community leaders attended the weekend festivities. The community relationships that helped to build the new center were strengthened in the actions that occurred shortly after the grand opening, as a result of the meetings. The Kirtland Kiwanis were the first to host an event in the new theater. Elementary school kids visited the gardens each spring and fall to learn about various plants and bugs, and following the encouragement of the senior center and community religious leaders, a canvas labyrinth was purchased. The labyrinth is rolled out each winter, and community residents are invited to use it as a form of meditation in the warm visitor center theater (the center is closed to the public during January and February). These small gestures have created a community space that residents now view as their own.

Advocate for the Preserving and Sharing of Your Community's Rich Heritage

Small museums have a tendency to measure their value to the community by the size of their actual site or organization. This terrible misconception can have a lasting negative impact on site morale. Small museums have an incredible opportunity based on their minimal staff and limited space. In most cases, small museums do not have to struggle with a bureaucracy paralyzed by tradition and red tape, such as typically exists in large institutions. If a site director wants to collaborate with the local high school as an advisor for the Interact Club, he or she can simply agree to devote the time and resources to the partnership rather than having to seek approval from a series of administrators, which could easily take weeks. Small museums also have the opportunity to expand outside their sites as a result of limited space for public programs.

Villa Finale, a historic site located in San Antonio, Texas, is beginning its legacy as a house museum by engaging the local community in historic preservation. This beautifully built 1876 Italianate mansion was once home to Walter Nold Mathis, a wealthy individual and avid collector of all things from houses to fine decorative arts from a variety of cultures. Recognizing the current house museum market and the probability of survival, the staff at Villa Finale gathered a committee of museum professionals, historians, Mathis family members, and staff from the National Trust for Historic Preservation to discuss the historic home's future. The brass tacks gathering made a number of discoveries, as well as created a clear direction for the mission and direction of the historic site. Sandra Smith, Villa Finale director, summarized the plan: "What we realized is that the only way our museum can survive is to not just look back, but to look forward as well. . . . A significant part of our mission will be to continue Mathis's neighborhood preservation work and advocacy by establishing a Center for Neighborhood Preservation, where residents of San Antonio's many diverse historic districts can learn to care for their homes through hands-on training and educational workshops. The Center will also encourage residents to play a role in developing the future of their neighborhoods."[8]

Liberty Hall's former director, Alma Blair, has continued to be an active voice in the collection and preservation of local history. Although the historic site focuses on the life and times of a particular nineteenth-century family, Blair expanded Liberty Hall's educational focus to include the preservation and sharing of Lamoni's history with the Smith family as an example of nineteenth-century Lamoni culture. Community residents, recognizing Blair's passion for public history, slowly began sharing historic pictures from their families' collections. Blair made scanned copies of the photos, newspapers, letters, and so forth, and used the information for traveling presentations at the local schools, assisted living homes, and local congregations. A number of local restaurants and travel centers have requested copies of Blair's collection for their businesses.

Liberty Hall does not have the resources or facilities to own and maintain the sizable archival collection; however, this does not prevent the staff from continuing to advocate for community preservation and education. The staff continues to give credit to the individual families.[9]

Liberty Hall's advocacy for preserving and sharing local history does not end with Blair's presentations. The local newspaper reserves an editorial column for the former site director's reflections on local history. Each week, Blair shares an interesting story, biographical sketch, or look back on Lamoni's collective past. Much of the information is derived from his traveling education programs, and each column draws a connection with the past that is relevant to Lamoni's future.

Perhaps it was Blair's emphasis on community history that provoked Lamoni's residents to protest the demolition of Herald Hall, a historic building once used as a print shop, school dormitory, and administrative offices for the local schools. After an extensive cost analysis of structural improvements, the local school district had decided to tear down Herald Hall in order to replace the historic structure with a modern office building. Residents and alumni alike voiced their concerns about the impact of the school district's decision. Blair and the staff at Liberty Hall assisted in facilitating community discussion and giving both sides ample opportunity to be heard. Ultimately, Herald Hall was demolished. However, prior to the demolition, Blair was given permission to document and photograph the historic structure. With the help of community funding, his records were published, and copies were sent to local families, libraries, and the state historic preservation office in Des Moines. Despite Liberty Hall's limited space, the volunteer staff's ambition for community education has no limitation.

In the case of the Kirtland Temple, volunteer and paid staff involvement in local organizations such as the Kirtland Kiwanis, Lake County Visitors Bureau, and Kirtland Ministerial Alliance opened a number of doors to local history advocacy and awareness. During the various gatherings for the community organizations, connections were created, and relationships were forged with fellow administrators from history organizations within the county. Out of these relationships, a variety of collaborative programs were developed from joint exhibits to special events and themed packaged tours like "Church, State and Plate," a packaged tour with the Lake County History Center that included special programs at the Kirtland Temple, James A. Garfield Presidential Home, and Lake Farmpark. The packaged tours allowed the Kirtland Temple to expand from its traditional audience into a new arena of history enthusiasts and philanthropists. It also gave the site an opportunity to showcase both the temple and the outreach services provided by the staff.

Political Advocacy and the Small Museum: Do Not Be Afraid to Reach Outside Your Walls

Small museum leaders should not be afraid to reach outside the walls of their organization to take an active role as political advocates for local preservation and education. A number of small museums across the country have expanded their community service at both the local and national levels. These initiatives are often accompanied by a new focus on protecting, tracking, and advocating for the community's historical assets, including the preservation of local stories and collections that are not owned by the historic sites and may never make it into the museum's collection. Simultaneously, the small museums have gained awareness and support from their community leaders. Mayors and city councilmen have become not only aware of the museums' existence but informed of their purpose and the essential service they provide to the larger community.

Perhaps the most influential role the Kirtland Temple has played in the past ten years has been the relationships created with Kirtland's civic leadership. The past three site directors have held a position on the cemetery board, including serving as board chair for a brief period. Regular attendance at civic meetings and community events has strengthened the relationship between the small museum and the city's leadership. The temple staff continued actively engaging the local library in creating small exhibit displays for the library's wall case each year. Rather than creating displays focused heavily on temple history, these volunteers expanded their educational focus to include a broader Kirtland history. Exhibits compared historic and contemporary Kirtland and invited community residents to share their photos with the staff at the temple. Other displays showcased historic reunions and community events on the temple grounds and a "Who's Who of Historic Kirtland." The small exhibit cases made a short period of Kirtland's history (the 1830s Kirtland Temple) seem rather relevant to the local community. Rather than focusing primarily on preserving and interpreting Mormon history, the site began expanding its focus to engage the locals in all aspects of preserving their shared past.

Slowly, the historic site and associated staff began to be perceived as local history entrepreneurs and "go-to" people for questions regarding local heritage. Outreach extended to the county parks level as park administrators began revisioning the interpretive message to best relate to a wider audience. Kirtland Temple staff acted as consultants in the integration of local history from the photograph/archive collection to basic approaches in historical interpretation. Soon temple volunteers were involved in park ranger classes and volunteer orientation. The services of the small historic site were spreading far outside temple properties at limited expense to the small museum. Slowly, the temple and its staff have emerged from a once limited historic place and period to become a center of local history where the people of Kirtland are encouraged to preserve and share their own individual heritages as part of a much greater community story.

The greatest compliment paid to the temple by the civic leaders of Kirtland stemmed from the personal relationships created and the leadership's awareness of the important role the temple played in enriching and

Photo 3.5. Cemetery Preservation: Kirtland Temple staff collaborates with the City Cemetery Board to advocate the preservation and interpretation of historic cemeteries in the Kirtland community. (Courtesy of Barbara Walden)

preserving local history. In 2000, with the assistance of local voters, a historic district was created and signs produced to signify the district's geographical location. The handmade signs produced by the city of Kirtland included an image of the Kirtland Temple. The temple was literally seen as an icon of Kirtland's history.

The Howard County Historical Society (HCHS) located in Kokomo, Indiana, is another excellent example of a small museum taking an active role in advocating for the needs of the community through civic leadership. Kelly Karickhoff, executive director, views the society's interaction with Kokomo's civic leadership less as political advocacy and more as "friend building."[10] The HCHS is a small museum making a significant impact on the preservation of local history. Under Karickhoff's leadership and an active governing board, it has collaborated with a number of organizations on projects as varied as developing educational programs and oral histories to building economic development for the county through the local county visitor and conventions bureau. The HCHS has an open-door policy with the community and invites use of its buildings as space for a variety of activities, from serving as office space for the local symphony and an accountant to hosting special events for the local mayor.

The secret to the HCHS's success in winning the support of its local leadership is twofold: first, an active and engaged board and, second, a willingness to open the doors of the historical society to the needs of the community. The HCHS's board includes twenty-one members with a variety of careers and experiences. The roots of the museum's active role in local leadership began when a former county councilman accepted a position on the HCHS board. He gave helpful insight into local government and political processes. He helped museum staff and fellow board members understand how local politicians processed community issues, as well as what was relevant to the goals and objectives of the local city council. This also caused the board to move from an internal focus on the museum and its historical properties to an external community focus. The board accepted ownership and began to invest in the museum as a landmark of the larger community. Karickhoff stated simply, "We wanted to be a centerpiece of community pride for Kokomo."[11]

The Howard County Historical Society has since become a visible part of the community in a number of ways. The museum hosts a luncheon for county officials during the budget and audit seasons. This simple event allows the HCHS to create an experience for the county's leadership at the community's museum. It is a continuous reminder of the HCHS's vision and mission while the county's political leaders are in the process of considering the museum's budget. The museum also hosts the mayor and city council throughout the year for a variety of activities. Each is a visual reminder of the essential role the museum plays in preserving the historic identity and culture of Kokomo.

When Kokomo's civic leaders are not at the museum, Karickhoff and her staff maintain the lines of communication with their local politicians through press releases, phone calls, and office visits. Their leaders are informed not only about the HCHS's special events but about research projects, community collaborations, and education programs. The museum staff continues to keep local

**Photo 3.6.   Civic Engagement: Encourage local congressmen and state represen-
tatives to use your site when promoting heritage areas and local tourism. (Courtesy of Barbara Walden)**

leaders informed about the history needs of the community, such as what history topics should be preserved through oral histories. The HCHS's direction
includes asking community leadership and neighbors the essential question,
"What is important to you?" By engaging with local leaders on what they perceive as important elements of Kokomo's story, the museum not only actively
engages its political leaders but gives them an opportunity to feel invested in the
museum's projects so that they financially and politically support them.

Overlooking the breathtaking shores of the winding Georges River, hundreds of miles away from the Indiana plains and the Howard County Historical
Society, stands Montpelier, the home of General Henry Knox. The General
Henry Knox Museum is an excellent example of a small museum actively engaged in political advocacy. Like General Knox himself, the museum began as
ordinary but developed into something extraordinary. The small staff and engaged board continue to take courageous and strategic actions to engage national
leaders on the importance of preserving and sharing the story of Montpelier.

Ellen Dyer, executive director of the General Henry Knox Museum, is the
first to admit that the secret to its advocacy success is an active and engaged
board of directors.[12] Like the board of the Howard County Historical Society,

the Knox Museum's board included a member who had experience working in government, in this case, as a personal assistant to the late Senator James Pickle of Texas. Although the congressman did not represent Thomaston, Maine, the board member's experience informed the Knox Museum board of the crucial role Maine's senators and congressmen needed to play in supporting the museum's mission.

With the support of her board, Dyer collaborated with Mount Vernon and the Society of the Cincinnati, and traveled to Washington, DC, to share the story of General Knox and the Knox Museum. Dyer and her museum colleagues spent three days visiting various congressional offices and strongly advocating for the museum in 2009. The trip resulted in a growing relationship with her local congresswoman, Chellie Pingree, and Maine's senator Susan Collins. Both the senator and the congresswoman are kept informed about the museum's activities, events, and educational programs. Both offices are well aware of the museum's vision and strategic plan. Dyer does not submit an Institute of Museum and Library Services grant application without informing her congressional and senatorial leaders. Although the museum's political engagement and advocacy has not translated into immediate financial support, Dyer and her staff feel a strong sense of moral support from their national leaders through communication and presence.

The Small Museum: A Universal "Center of Community Life"?

Small museums across the country, whether in the cornfields of Iowa or the rolling hills of northeastern Ohio, are becoming significant places of community engagement. Local museums are places where civic leaders and neighborhood families are encouraged to ask the difficult questions and experience the depth and meaning of a shared community story. Our continuing challenge as small museum curators, administrators, board members, and volunteers is to channel the powerful potential of history to improve the unique communities in which we live. Small museum leaders must be willing to roll up their sleeves as they immerse themselves in dialogue with their neighbors. We must be willing to go the extra mile to address the needs of our local communities in an open-minded fashion with the understanding that our institutions do not have all the answers. Through the spirit of collaboration with other like-minded individuals and institutions, the needs of our neighbors and larger community residents will be served.

As interpreters and collections managers, we continue to form public conscience as storytellers, memory activists, lesson teachers, and "keepers of the fire." As Ruth J. Abram, founder and president of the Lower East Side Tenement

Photo 3.7. Community Festival: Small museum staffs often roll up their sleeves and go the extra mile to meet the needs of the community. Here an intern at the Kirtland Temple is volunteering off hours at a local festival to raise awareness and funding for the local youth programs and services. (Courtesy of Barbara Walden)

Museum in New York City, so eloquently summarized to her colleagues from the Museums of Conscience, "We hope to make explicit what has been merely implicit: our sites are important, not because of the stories they tell, but rather because they hold lessons so powerful that they could improve our lives if we would just listen. Such is the power of history."[13] Such is the power of our small museums.

Notes

1. Over two hundred denominations have sprung from the original Mormon Church once headquartered in Kirtland, Ohio. The largest of these is the Church of Jesus Christ of Latter-Day Saints, headquartered in Salt Lake City, Utah. The Kirtland Temple is owned and operated by the Community of Christ, headquartered in Independence, Missouri.

2. For more information about Jeffrey Lundgren and the Avery family murders, see Pete Earley, *Prophet of Death: The Mormon Blood-Atonement Killings* (New York: William Morrow and Co., 1991). The cover of the Earley book is an additional example of the Kirtland Temple's damaged public image and the negative community relationships following the Kirtland murders. The only image that appears on the cover of the book is an enlarged image of the Kirtland Temple. Additional information on the media's portrayal of the Kirtland murders may be found in the *Cleveland Plain Dealer*'s archives (www.plaindealer.com).

3. John Durel and Anita Nowery Durel, "A Golden Age for Historic Properties," *History News* 62, no. 4 (summer 2007): 9.

4. Liberty Hall, located in Lamoni, Iowa, was once home to Joseph Smith III and his family from 1881 to 1905. For more information, see "Joseph Smith III's Liberty Hall," Community of Christ, www.cofchrist.org/lamoni/default.asp (accessed May 30, 2011).

5. Interview with Martha McKain, site coordinator of Joseph Smith III's Liberty Hall, February 2010. Interview notes are in the author's possession.

6. David W. Young et al., "Not Dead Yet: Historic Sites Providing Community Leadership," *History News* 64, no. 3 (summer 2009): 19.

7. Young et al., "Not Dead Yet," 19.

8. Young et al., "Not Dead Yet," 20.

9. Interview with Alma Blair from Joseph Smith III's Liberty Hall, February 2010. Interview notes are in the author's possession.

10. Interview with Kelly Karickhoff, executive director of Howard County Historical Society, July 2010. Interview notes are in the author's possession.

11. Interview with Karickhoff.

12. Interview with Ellen Dyer, executive director of the General Henry Knox Museum, July 2010. Interview notes are in the author's possession.

13. Ruth J. Abram, "Using the Past to Shape the Future: New Concepts for Historic Sites," *Museum International* 53, no. 1 (January–March 2001): 9.

CHAPTER FOUR
ACCESSIBILITY IS FOR EVERYONE
Kat Burkhart

For most museums and historic sites, sharing their story with as many people as possible is their primary goal. Visitors seek out sites and experiences that accommodate them and their families. That means Grandma and Grandpa and the little kids in diapers and everyone in between. Some of them do not see that well, or hear that well, or even pay attention that well. They may or may not be part of the officially designated sight-, hearing-, or mobility-impaired crowds. Does your site accommodate any or all of these groups? Can your site handle baby strollers and wheelchairs; the sight, hearing, and mobility impaired; or the tired parents and grandparents who just want to sit for a minute? Making all these groups feel welcome and wanting to return is what accessibility is all about, and it can be done in museums of all sizes, including your small museum.

What Is Accessibility?

In this chapter, the word "accessibility" refers to the degree to which museum services or environments are available and welcoming to as many people as possible. Though the word is often used to focus on people with disabilities and their right of access to goods and services, accessibility in small museums is about your inviting people to visit and being able to share your story with them. Wheelchairs are, of course, part of the accessibility equation, but there is a great deal more to accessibility that is frequently overlooked. Many different types of barriers keep people from visiting a site or make their visit difficult or uncomfortable. This chapter attempts to cover accessibility of all types. It is possible for small museums to make small, gradual changes, often with little or no additional cost, that will make the site much more welcoming to all visitors.

What Is the Americans with Disabilities Act?

After many years of work by those advocating for the disabled, the Americans with Disabilities Act (ADA) was enacted to remove barriers between those with a disability and goods and services, including museums. As with most laws, following this one is not optional. The ADA has only been around since 1990, and it was generally assumed that making buildings, as well as goods and services, fully accessible would take time. More than twenty years later, expectations for accessibility are rising.

TEXTBOX 4.1

A CAUTIONARY TALE

The International Spy Museum in Washington, DC, is not a small museum, but its former lack of accessibility for people who are blind or have low vision and those who are deaf or hard of hearing made national headlines, and that is relevant to all museums. A patron claimed that the museum did not make reasonable accommodations, such as handouts in Braille or large print or guides trained in providing accessible tours.

In 2008, the Department of Justice and the International Spy Museum reached an agreement to address its accessibility issues.[1] This decision will have far-reaching influence across the museum world and is something all museum staff should be aware of and understand: It is possible for a museums to be sued for not addressing accessibility. Individuals with disabilities and their families want full access to enjoy goods and services and will continue to advocate for this civil right.

The Spy Museum is now much more accessible. It features tactile objects or audio components in many places, offers a text-based map and description of these points in advance, a tactile map of the museum's floor plan, and audio-described tours and orientations included in the price of admission. It also has text for audio presentations placed near the locations and a system that triggers captions on videos throughout the museum. It offers sign language and other interpreter services with advance notice. All floors, exhibits, and restrooms are accessible by wheelchairs.[2]

Notes

1. "Fact Sheet: Settlement Agreement between Department of Justice and International Spy Museum," ADA Home Page, June 3, 2008, www.ada.gov/spymuseum fctsht.html (accessed May 12, 2011).

2. "Accessibility," International Spy Museum, www.spymuseum.org/accessibility (accessed May 12, 2011).

How Do I Comply with the ADA?

The ADA is a complicated law, and how it applies to your particular situation is beyond the scope of this chapter. (As in all issues of law, consulting an experienced lawyer is strongly recommended.) However, do not fear. At the end of this chapter, you will find an annotated resource list of online and print materials about ADA compliance. The list is broken into multiple categories, including items for reference, in-depth resources, and checklists you can start using today.

Accessibility goes beyond ADA compliance, though that is also very important. Accessibility is an attitude. It is a perspective on how we choose to approach the delivery of our services to meet the needs of as many people as possible.

What Does This Mean for Staff and Volunteers at Small Museums?

As programmatic ideas and exhibits are discussed while planning for the future and especially during any sort of renovation or updating, accessibility should be a factor in what the museum chooses to do. When something breaks or wears out or you just want to make small changes in the interpretation, you have the opportunity to make changes in a more accessible direction. When your goal is accessibility, every brochure, every website, and, yes, every tour may need updating or revision on a regular basis. Museums that do not at least attempt to make their sites somewhat accessible run the risk of losing credibility, losing visitors, and, in the worst case, losing lawsuits (see textbox 4.1).

Why Is Accessibility Important?

If the museum or site is accessible, everyone will benefit and find the place more welcoming. Everyone appreciates extra seating in the galleries or on the tour. Easily read signage or text panels are a positive for people of all ages and vision levels. The baby boom generation has just begun to retire and over the next few decades will become an even greater target audience for tourism. This is one reason to look at your museum now and to make plans and set goals for the future with regard to accessibility. Demographics in the United States are changing, and the percentage of the population over the age of sixty-five is growing quickly: "In 2000, the 65-and-older population comprised 35.0 million people. Within this group, 18.5 million people or 53 percent were aged 65 to 74, 12.3 million or 35 percent were aged 75 to 84, and 4.2 million or 12 percent were aged 85 and over."[1] The bulk of the American population right now is between the ages of eighteen and sixty-five, but the baby boomers are getting older, there are a lot of them, and they are often the most frequent visitors to and strongest supporters of museums and historic sites. While members of this age group are often targeted as museum goers, they will restrict their visits to museums that can and will accommodate them now and as they age.

Accessibility is something to think about in the present as well as for the future. What incremental improvements can you make over time to improve access to your site for everyone? Do not forget to include accessibility options for families; if the site is wheelchair accessible, then it can be stroller accessible. Having a place to sit, change diapers, or nurse babies can make a great deal of difference to a family visiting museums. Many families have multigenerational concerns that need to be addressed for their comfort and for site and staff safety. If a site makes small changes as it can afford them, in ten years it should be much more accessible and more welcoming to all.

If you had sixty seconds to explain to your board why you need to address accessibility now, you might make the following arguments:

1. Making the museum or site accessible to individuals with disabilities increases your potential visitor pool and creates a better experience for everyone.
2. Most museums and historic sites are looking for more visitors and to be (or remain) a vital part of the community. Welcoming a diverse audience that includes people with disabilities will enhance your community standing and increase the value of your mission. (And you can advertise it!)
3. It is the law. The ADA prohibits discrimination on the basis of disability in employment, state and local government, public accommodations, commercial facilities, transportation, and tele-communications.[2]

When you bring up the topic of accessibility, you may hear, "It's so complicated" and "We just can't afford to be accessible." Accessibility is an always-changing, multilayered spectrum, but that does not make it impossible for small museums. To avoid getting overwhelmed, break overall accessibility down into smaller pieces and ask for help.

Accessibility and Mission

How your museum handles accessibility depends on its mission. The relationship between the structure or architecture and the mission of the institution is important to acknowledge. Evaluate this relationship and determine how important the building's architecture really is to the mission and the institution.

There are alternatives to direct accessibility, including, but not limited to, making a portion of the site accessible, such as the first floor or a separate building, where visitors can watch a video of a tour, narrated and captioned, and see or feel maps of the site and artifacts or reproductions.

For example, the architecture of the Molly Brown House Museum in Denver, Colorado, is core to its mission of historic preservation. Designed and built in 1889, the Molly Brown House Museum re-creates the lavish turn-of-the-century lifestyle of the "unsinkable" Margaret (Molly) and J. J. Brown. The architecture of this once private home is an important part of its story. On the other hand, although the Carnegie Museum of Montgomery County in Crawfordsville, Indiana, is located in a historic building, public access is paramount to the historic integrity of the building. A public building from its beginning, it was restored and adapted to be a community museum, not primarily for the sake of preservation. This is a spectrum, not an either-or, but it is something to think about and discuss with the staff and board. Does your institution's mission specifically mention the site's historic structure and building preservation?

Once you have a good sense of how accessibility relates to your mission, you are ready to examine your museum carefully to determine where accessibility issues exist and what you can do to resolve them.

Assessing Your Site: Performing an Accessibility Audit

In examining challenges and possible solutions for accessibility, you will need to consider a wide variety of areas. Use the Accessibility Matrix (textbox 4.3) to organize your efforts to audit your site. Review the items listed as they apply to your specific situation. Make whatever changes you need; the matrix is meant to be a starting point. Museums vary widely in size, architecture, period, location, and pretty much every other way possible. All museum structures and sites are unique and present their own challenges.

How do you know what your site needs to do to become more accessible? It is often difficult to look at your own site with fresh eyes, in a critical and unbiased way. Bringing in someone new, someone who is not familiar with the site and the interpretation, can provide that critical perspective. Museums often bring in outsiders for strategic planning and for consultation on utilities, grounds, and many other things. Financial audits commonly take place with outside personnel. Auditing accessibility is much the same. The museum volunteers and staff, including the board of directors, are probably not experts on accessibility and the laws and resources that apply. Someone from the outside, who has an interest in improving accessibility, can be very valuable. Additionally, outsiders will often notice things and bring up challenges (and possible solutions) that museum staff will overlook because of their great familiarity with the site. For example, if you have worked at the site for ten years, you may have noticed the heaviness of the front door on your first day, but after that it became part of your work routine.

Gathering the Team

The audit process will take time and should ideally be a team effort. (Even one additional person can still make a difference!) The first step is developing your team. Ask for advice and collaborate with local groups and organizations. To get input on the site or the tour, talk to local or regional schools for the deaf and blind. Local public school counselors may be able to visit the site and talk to the museum staff. Service organizations that assist people with disabilities in developing job skills, socialization skills, and finding employment may also be interested

---

TEXTBOX 4.2

CASE STUDY: TESTING ACCESSIBILITY

As part of a general assessment, the Carnegie Museum of Montgomery County staff invited a local young man, who is blind, to tour the museum and give his input on the exhibitions and layout. The museum is wheelchair accessible, has an elevator, and has hosted multiple groups in wheelchairs. Bringing in a blind visitor tested another aspect of museum accessibility. The experiment was meant to help clarify the museum's strengths and weaknesses. The staff planned for his arrival as they would any other tour arranged in advance.

His response was quite telling about his expectations. He was very surprised to have enjoyed himself.

> It was a museum, so I wasn't psyched. I was afraid they were going to overcompensate for my disability and make me feel like an idiot, but they didn't. The exhibits were interesting. I liked feeling the torpedo cover, the lightning generator, and the switchboard. The switchboard was fun. The staff was helpful and friendly.

This successful trial encouraged museum staff to incorporate multiple sensory experiences into most of the galleries. In striving to include as many people as possible, hands-on activities, sounds, and smells are used often in the interpretation. Evaluation of placement of aisles and walkways in the exhibits occurs on a more frequent basis as the exhibits change.

in bringing their clients to the museum and can provide feedback to the staff about what works well and what does not. Nursing homes often have activity directors on staff; ask them to visit the site and to provide feedback, or perhaps they have some residents who would love to visit the museum or have the museum staff show a video of the tour at their facility. This could also be a great opportunity to reach out to local groups with whom you might not have regular communications.

One of the easiest and most cost-effective ways to find out if there is a problem—or, if you know there is one, to address it—is to ask people to come in and test your site. It can be difficult to admit that the site does not accommodate everyone; however, the solution lies in finding out who you can accommodate and what can be done to make the site more enjoyable for everyone.

The Accessibility Matrix

There is no one way to make every site accessible, but each ability category can be measured against the marketing, the site (particularly the entrances and parking), the tour or exhibits, the restrooms and gift shop, and any other part of the museum intended for the public.

You can do this for the staff side of the museum as well if you have the time and energy! Take a single ability and test the site. Examine its strengths and weaknesses, and document them.

This matrix is intended as an example. Feel free to add rows and columns in whatever category needed. Some museums have parking; others do not. You may want to add "Outreach Programs" as an option or "Gardens" if your site has them. Ask one of your community contacts to try out every aspect of your site and tell you about his or her reactions and first impressions. Then try it again with a

---

TEXTBOX 4.3

ACCESSIBILITY MATRIX

	Marketing	Entrances and Parking	Exhibits and Tours	Gift Shop and Restrooms
Hearing impaired				
Visually impaired				
Mobility impaired				
Other				

different ability. After you complete the audit using this matrix, bring it to a team meeting and brainstorm about what can be done, when, how, and by whom. Make lists about what you can do right away, what changes take money (how much they will cost), and who should make them. In the short term, look at the upcoming schedule of exhibits, activities, and programs to see what you can do to be a bit more accommodating without spending any additional money. In the long term, consider what you wish you could do to the site to make it more accessible. Ask yourself and your team, "What is stopping us from making the change?" and "How can we work to overcome this?" Asking and answering these questions is the first step toward making your site more accessible and a better place for everyone.

For example, developing a large-print brochure might be a small project if you already have a brochure on your computer, whereas a change to the website might take a bit longer, and a physical change to part of the site or tour will likely take even more time and money. But you can break this process down into manageable tasks, and it is okay if doing so itself takes some time. Assessing accessibility does not have to be accomplished all in one week—but it could be if the team were motivated enough and had the time. Sometimes it helps to just get it all done at once if the team is amenable. Do what works best for you and your team.

Topics to Include in Your Site Audit

These topics do not make up an exhaustive list for every museum, but they do represent some basic areas that all museums should consider, and they correspond with the columns in the Accessibility Matrix. See textbox 4.4 for other potential points of discussion for your site audit.

Marketing

Begin at the beginning. The perception of accessibility is almost as important as actually having accessible accommodations. Examine your marketing materials and strategy. Marketing materials bring visitors to the site. These include brochures, rack cards, newsletters, websites, and other promotional items. If the museum is accessible, this fact should be mentioned in the brochures and on the website. Look at the promotional photographs of the site. If steep steps or big doors are featured prominently because of the building's architecture, add text or images to highlight the accessibility of the site.

For example, the Carnegie Museum of Montgomery County is a small museum located in a public commercial building. The building is over one hundred years old, but during its time as a public library, it was renovated to include wheelchair accessibility with the addition of an elevator and a street-level entrance. This building is handicapped accessible, but does it look it? Take a look at photos 4.1 and 4.2, and then compare them to photo 4.3.

Photos 4.1 and 4.2. These are the types of photograph that might be used to promote the Carnegie Museum of Montgomery County, *which is wheelchair accessible.* This is what most people see when they are walking or driving by the museum. It looks imposing and not accessible at all. Many potential visitors call to ask if they must climb the stairs.

Photo 4.3. This image presents a completely different view, and highlights the accessibility of the site to the general public. This does not need to be the primary image on a brochure or website, but it could be a helpful reminder near the hours, group tour information, or directions section of a publication.

The Molly Brown House Museum in Denver, Colorado, does an excellent job of describing its accessibility on the museum's website and in its promotional materials. Because the architecture and historical accuracy are very important to the mission and integrity of the building and there are many stairs, the Molly Brown House Museum has worked to inform and accommodate visitors, although it has not added ramps or elevators to the main building. Located in the downtown area, the museum has no room to expand the physical footprint of the site to become more accessible. Instead, it utilizes the existing carriage house and describes in its marketing how accommodations for visitors can be made with advanced notice. The museum also runs programs in the accessible carriage house located behind the main house, which includes a marked handicapped parking space.

Here is an excerpt from the Molly Brown House Museum's website: "The Molly Brown House Museum will strive to provide any special accommodations you may require. Please contact us in advance for these arrangements." This is the first thing to add to your marketing materials. It means, "We want you to visit the site, and we will try to work with you." As figure 4.1 shows, the Web page on accessibility from the Molly Brown House Museum website is upfront about the many steps that are a part of the tour, but the museum also indicates that it will try to work with potential visitors.[3] Making an effort is the most important part of accessibility.

Facility Information and Handicapped Accessibility

There are no lunch facilities on the property. The Museum Store offers bottled refreshments and light snacks only. There are many restaurants within walking distance of the Museum. You may also eat sack lunches on our grounds, the Capitol building grounds 3 blocks west of the Museum, or at Civic Center Park, 5 blocks west of the Museum.

The Museum is a multi-story, Victorian-era home constructed in 1889 and as a result is not fully accessible to all persons with disabilities.
- **The historic house museum is not wheelchair accessible.**
- Walking apparatus are permissible in the museum.
- "Touch" tours are available to the sight impaired with advanced notice.
- Access to the property and museum space requires navigating stairs.
- Tours of the museum last approximately 45 minutes and require short periods of walking and stair-climbing and longer periods of standing.
- Certified dogs are allowed in the museum only when utilized for assisted care.

The Carriage House Visitor's Center and Museum Store is handicapped accessible.
- The Visitor's Center located in the Carriage House to the rear of the museum site is wheelchair and handicap accessible from the one handicap parking space adjacent to the Carriage House (a permit must be displayed).
- Alternate tours can be provided within the Visitor's Center space including a documentary video about Margaret Brown and her 1889 home and other visual materials relating to the historic house museum.

The Molly Brown House Museum will strive to provide any special accommodations you may require. Please contact us in advance for these arrangements.

Figure 4.1. The Molly Brown House website, Accessibility Web page (www .mollybrown.org/visit-us/accessibility/)

Entrances and Parking

Exhibits, tours, and programming are obviously core to your mission, and all depend on visitors getting to your site. Marketing of the site or museum can be excellent, and you can have the best exhibits and programs in the world, but if potential visitors have trouble getting in the door, your efforts will be wasted.

If possible, designate and mark at least one space of the parking area for the handicapped. You may be required by law to provide a certain number of handicapped spaces depending on the number of parking spaces you control. Find out who is in charge of the streets surrounding your site (city, county, state, or federal government). Who controls the sign permits? Who repairs and maintains the roads? How quickly and easily parking can be made more accessible—and your ability then to promote that fact to your visitors—will depend on the rules and regulations of those in charge. (Consult the resource list at the end of this chapter or talk to your city or town zoning or planning commission for more information.)

If your visitors are constantly arriving at the wrong door, you may need to add signs. Hopefully your visitors can see the front door or entrance to your site from where they park or, if walking, orient themselves to your property. If not, start with a sign indicating where the accessible and other entries are.

If visitors are often confused about which door is the main entrance or where they are supposed to go first, a sign can address this immediately. It will not cost much and can drastically improve the experience for both staff and visitors.

Photo 4.4. Stairs are a major part of the stunning architecture of the Molly Brown House. (Courtesy of the Molly Brown House Museum)

At the Carnegie Museum of Montgomery County, the flagpole was moved to flank the accessible front entrance. This helped to accentuate the street-level entrance. Additionally, signs were placed in the windows of the street-level entrance encouraging people to visit. Large-print signs were added in the windows of the old main entrance at the top of the stairs to deter people from climbing the entire flight only to have to turn around and go back down to the main entrance to enter the museum. (The original entrance to the building at the top of the stairs is currently used as a fire exit and cannot be blocked.) These signs were made using the museum's computer and copier—a minor expense that has made a significant positive difference.

The Exhibit

Most museums use labels or text panels as part of their interpretation. There are rules and suggested sizes and colors for accessible printed museum labels. Use at least an eighteen-point font size. Keep the font and the colors simple, and utilize white space so that the text is not in one large block. Use sans serif or simple serif fonts, and keep the fonts consistent throughout the exhibit. Serifs are used in "old-fashioned" and script fonts. These can be difficult to read if used as a text or label font. If you really want to use serif fonts, reserve them for the titles and make the font extra large.

What does 18 point look like? Like this. No smaller. *Not this.*

Keep label text brief; use less than one hundred words per label, and always use high-contrast colors. Black and white work well for most people because they are high contrast. If you use different colors, make sure they contrast well and are easy to read. Creating easy-to-read labels for those with impaired vision will help other visitors, such as children, busy parents, and those with limited English. Determine how far away from the label the visitor will be and increase the size of the label text accordingly.

Use blank space to separate sections of text clearly on text panels, and keep the language direct and to the point. Make sure that the background is not busy or cluttered. View your labels from different heights; if seated in a wheelchair, you should be able to read the entire label easily. You should also be able to read the labels whether you are very tall or very short. If the local public library has a substantial, frequently checked-out selection of large-print materials, perhaps your site should increase the overall font size of its labels. Not many complaints are made because the font size is too big.

Lighting can improve or hinder the visitor experience. Overhead lighting should provide general illumination, with spot lighting on certain elements. Make sure that visitors are not blinded by bright lights from either natural sources or from light fixtures. Pay attention to the shadows and glare that lighting can cast to complicate or obstruct viewing of text panels or objects. For natural lighting, shadows or glare may change with the seasons; so check periodically throughout the year as different lighting and shadows might transform the visual aspects of the exhibit.

The Guided Tour

Make sure all staff and volunteers are trained to speak loudly and clearly and to watch their groups for signs of inattention or fatigue. Tour guides or docents should speak facing the visitors as often as possible. They should repeat questions asked by other visitors so that everyone in the group can follow the conversation. Not all disabilities are obvious, but an engaged guide can often spot who in the group might need a little extra help without making a fuss.

Again, consider the lighting. The place where the tour guide stands may have great lighting (as it should), but stand in your visitors' shoes and make sure that there are no blinding lights or glares.

Remember, if visitors are comfortable, they are much more likely to listen to what guides or interpreters have to say and to take their time digesting the information presented. Uncomfortable people, of all ages and abilities, do not have much fun at museums and will not want to return.

Having places to sit during a tour is usually simple and cost-effective. It is, however, important to distinguish where visitors are allowed to sit. Keeping visitors on their feet for the better part of an hour is asking a lot. Most will not need to sit the entire time but may need to take breaks. Museums can do this in various ways; providing folding stools or clearly marked chairs breaks up the tour into

Photo 4.5. The Tenement Museum uses visual aids such as enlarged photos, enlarged reproductions of primary source materials (e.g., letters), and printed copies of the tour guide script for each room. (Photo by Keiko Niwa, courtesy of Lower East Side Tenement Museum)

more manageable periods of standing. At the beginning of a tour, describe what it entails. Standing, climbing, walking—all should be discussed if extensive. The Molly Brown House Museum mentions on its website under "Accessibility," "Did you know the Museum has nine flights of stairs throughout the house?"[4] This is a helpful way to let visitors understand what to expect on the tour.

Restrooms and Gift Shop

Seating areas should be placed around the gift shop and restrooms at a minimum. Even if seating is provided throughout the site, make sure the seating near the gift shop and restrooms is ample, as this is where people most often have to wait.

Simple things like replacing the knobs or handles on restroom doors with more accessible latches can make a serious improvement for all museum visitors. Find hardware that you can manipulate with your closed fist. Visit a local public building and use an accessible restroom. Notice the fixtures on the doors and the handles on the faucet. Visit a few places, such as the local public library, the post office, the grocery store, and any other essential place in your community. Ask how much the accessible hardware costs to install and how long it has been there. Find out if grants were applied for and received. Local hardware stores should be able to assist you in your search for accessible handles and knobs, as well as premade signs to label restrooms.

Accessibility Is Possible for Small Museums!

Keep the Accessibility Matrix handy and visible to the staff and board. Keep the to-do lists where they will not be overlooked. After you bring in people from the outside, keep in touch with them and provide updates about the site's progress. Start with the simple and cheap items with an eye to the future. Know how accessibility fits into the museum's mission, budget, and strategic plan. Do the little things as you can afford them, but always be on the lookout for opportunities to increase visitor access.

Here is a short list of what most small museums can do immediately to increase the minimum level of accessibility to structures and sites. Some things are quite simple; others will take more time. This is not a comprehensive list; add to it or change it with ideas particular to your site from your accessibility audit.

For Individuals Who Are Blind or Have Low Vision
- Provide large-print maps, gallery guides, or models of the structure, site, and grounds.

ACCESSIBILITY AUDIT: POINTS OF DISCUSSION

- Are the marketing and promotional materials inviting to all people?
- Are video, audio, or downloadable PDFs of exhibits or tours available on the website?
- Can viewers change the font size on the website?
- Are videos on the website and at the physical site subtitled?
- Do you offer anything printed in more than one language? Large print?
- Can visitors see the front door or main entrance from where they are parked?
- Do signs tell visitors where to park and where to find the entrance?
- Is the door to the main entrance heavy or hard to open?
- Is there an accessible entrance separate from the main entrance?
- Can the visitors navigate the entrance and find the bathrooms and gift shop easily?
- Is the place to buy tickets obvious and well marked?
- Do visitors often come to the wrong door?
- Do visitors often leave family members or friends in the car or on the first floor?
- Are visitors sitting and leaning on artifacts?
- Are visitors too tired to buy anything in the gift shop after the tour?
- Do visitors need to put on their glasses to read the labels?
- How welcoming is the gift shop?
- Do visitors keep their coats on for the entire tour?
- Are there places to sit or rest during the tour?
- How long is the standard tour of the site?
- Are visitors expected to stand for the whole tour?

- Provide a staff member or trained volunteer to read labels in all exhibitions or to verbally provide interpretation (not just to point to an exhibit but to describe it!).
- Provide a representative sample of objects, models, or reproductions of objects to communicate the primary themes of the exhibitions for tactile examination, along with audio or verbal description. (Recorded audio is okay; a live person is best.)

- Provide copies of photos that can be examined closely and handled by visitors.
- Keep pathways, doorways, and walkways clear and well marked.

For Individuals Who Are Deaf or Hard of Hearing

- Provide written text of all audio presentations, including guided tours, or make it available in electronic form so that it can be downloaded to users' electronic devices.
- Find a local provider of sign language to have on call for those who can schedule appointments in advance. Mention on museum materials that this service is available if tours are scheduled in advance.

For Everyone

- Display information about the availability of these auxiliary aids and services on the website and in brochures as well as other publications.
- Ensure that all new construction and alterations will be accessible.

Photo 4.6. An American Sign Language (ASL) interpreter can be hired to accommodate tours booked in advance. (Photo by Keiko Niwa, courtesy of Lower East Side Tenement Museum)

Photo 4.7. Lower East Side Tenement Museum. (Photo by Keiko Niwa, courtesy of Lower East Side Tenement Museum)

- Have places for visitors (and volunteers) to sit, even if only metal folding chairs.
- Educate staff and volunteers on how to handle requests from visitors, focusing on being truthful and clear but making sure that there is something of value to offer.
- Post signs allowing guide dogs or assistance animals.
- If your site has a website, investigate adding additional information and adjustable font-size options for the text components.

115

CASE STUDY: TENEMENT MUSEUM, NEW YORK CITY

While not the smallest of institutions, the Tenement Museum has made its site as accessible as possible in very reasonable, affordable ways that small museums can emulate. Built on Manhattan's Lower East Side in 1863, this tenement apartment building was home to nearly seven thousand working-class immigrants. The museum tells their stories. Historic buildings like this one are not easy to make wheelchair accessible but can often readily accommodate visitors with hearing or visual and some mobility impairments.

For visitors with the inability to stand for long periods, the Tenement Museum provides three folding chairs in every apartment on the tour. These are conspicuously modern, metal chairs so that visitors do not confuse the period furniture with the chairs they can sit on.

For visitors with visual impairments, hardcopies of primary source materials are passed around on every tour. These are held in front of a tour group, where they are easy to see, and also passed around the group for people to look at individually. High-resolution scans or color copies of primary source material can be laminated or inserted into page protectors. Additionally, copies of the tour guide's script are printed in a large, sans serif font and also passed around.

The cost to create these aids and add folding chairs is minimal. The museum also offers touch tours, American Sign Language tours, virtual tours, and a great deal more. The website has schedules of special tours and information about accessibility and how the museum is working to include as many visitors as possible.[1]

Note

1. "Accessible Tours and Services," Lower East Side Tenement Museum, www. tenement.org/vizinfo_ada.html (accessed May 12, 2011).

Conclusion

Now that you have an understanding of accessibility, every exhibit and tour, and especially any construction, can be examined with accessibility in mind. By making the museum directly accessible to all people, the museum will become, or continue to be, a vital part of the community. While you may not be able to address all the items identified in your accessibility audit right away, continued effort will be appreciated. Identify the long-term changes and include them in your plans for the future.

The old adage is true: Keep trying. Small things add up and can make the site a much more welcoming place for everyone. The overarching goal is to have a comfortable and enjoyable site where all people feel welcome to visit and return again and again.

Resources

Literally thousands of pages, both in print and online, focus on accessibility as it relates to small museums. They can be intimidating and time-consuming to wade through all at once. Because I know that you are short on money and time, these introductory resources are grouped by how you might use them:

- *Checklists:* quick-start items to use for assessment
- *References:* items to bookmark, print out, or have on hand as reference material
- *In-depth materials:* topical resources for teams or boards to review
- *Basic ADA:* excerpts from the actual law for perspective or in case someone asks

The following resources are mostly websites and Web pages because much of this information is updated frequently. If you prefer books, call these organizations and see what they currently offer or check things out from your local library. Not all resources will be helpful to all groups. Use what works best for you. Webinars are widely available and a great option if you cannot attend a workshop. They are relatively inexpensive and offered frequently.

Checklists

Disability Rights Section. "The Americans with Disabilities Act Checklist for Readily Achievable Barrier Removal: Checklist for Existing Facilities, version 2.1." ADA.gov. 1995. www.ada.gov/racheck.pdf. If you are not in a historic structure, start with this checklist.

National Endowment for the Arts. "The Arts and Humanities Accessibility Checklist." National Endowment for the Arts. www.nea.gov/resources/Accessibility/Planning/Step6.pdf. Part of the larger *Accessibility Planning and Resource Guide for Cultural Administrators*, this incredibly comprehensive, fifty-one-page checklist will give you an idea of what you can aspire to.

U.S. General Services Administration. "Accessibility Checklist for Historic Properties." U.S. General Services Administration. http://w3.gsa.gov/web/p/HPTP.NSF/gsagovAllProceduresDisplay/0110009S. If you are in a historic structure, this is the checklist for you.

References

ADA National Network (www.adata.org): The ADA National Network provides information, guidance, and training on the Americans with Disabilities Act. Call (800) 949–4232. For documents, visit www.adaportal.org; for training, visit www.adacourse.org.

American Association of Museums (www.aam-us.org): This is a good place to start to see what references will be helpful to your specific site and questions. Type "accessibility" into the search box on the website; some content is available to the general public and some only to AAM members.

Association of Science-Technology Centers (www.astc.org/resource/access/index.htm): This website covers a broad range of accessibility information, including legal background, best practices, an access survey, training, publications, and an electronic newsletter (*EXCHANGE*) that addresses specific museum areas, such as gift shops, information desks, and family restrooms.

National Center on Accessibility (www.ncaonline.org): This site focuses on promoting access and inclusion for people with disabilities in parks, recreation and tourism. The NCA has a unique perspective as it relates to museums, because of its cooperative agreement with the National Park Service. They have many resources, including lists of publications and videos on the website.

Salmen, John P. S., ed. *Everyone's Welcome.* Washington, DC: American Association of Museums, 1998. With funding from the Department of Justice, the AAM Americans with Disabilities Act Project developed a comprehensive accessibility resource package, including a manual and video, promoting and explaining the concept of universal design (available through the AAM bookstore).

U.S. Department of Justice, ADA Home Page (www.ada.gov): This is the "everything you could possibly want to know" website on the Americans with Disabilities Act and the details of the law. Spend some time to get familiar with the site so you know how to find things that are relevant to your work as you progress. Some material may be available on CD or as hard copy by request. Highlights for the small museum include

- *ADA Guide for Small Businesses*;
- Title III regulations;
- *Title III Technical Assistance Manual*; and
- *ADA Standards for Accessible Design*.

In-Depth Materials

Art Education for the Blind's Art beyond Sight, Bringing Art & Culture to All (www.artbeyondsight.org): This site will help you think about what you can do to increase access for visually impaired visitors, even if you have nothing to do with art.

Design for Accessibility: A Cultural Administrator's Handbook. Washington DC: National Assembly of State Arts Agencies, 2003. Available at www.nea.gov/resources/accessibility/pubs/DesignAccessibility/DesignAccess.pdf. At 171 pages, this is quite a read, but it is a good resource to have bookmarked or to skim for ideas and perspective. It is fairly user-friendly, and as it is a PDF, you can print it out if you want.

Jester, Thomas C., and Sharon C. Park. "Making Historic Properties Accessible." National Park Service, Preservation Briefs 32. www.nps.gov/history/hps/tps/briefs/brief32.htm. At about twelve pages, this preservation brief is a good place to start if historic preservation is a top priority. It also covers historic landscapes.

NEA Office for AccessAbility, National Endowment for the Arts (www.nea.gov/resources/accessibility/index.html): This website covers a wide variety of topics, with an eye to the arts and arts facilities, but sections on universal design and website accessibility will apply to all.

Smithsonian Institution. *Guidelines for Universal Design of Exhibits.* Washington, DC: Smithsonian Institution, 2000. Available at http://accessible.si.edu/gfude.htm. An introduction to the concept of universal design with concrete examples includes a discussion of visual, tactile, and audio experiences, as well as the physical environment.

Basic ADA

ADA Title III, Subpart A—General Excerpts (www.ada.gov/regs2010/titleIII_2010/titleIII_2010_regulations.htm#subparta).

§ 36.104 Definitions

"*Disability* means, with respect to an individual, a physical or mental impairment that substantially limits one or more of the major life activities of such individual; a record of such an impairment; or being regarded as having such an impairment."

"*Place of public accommodation* means a facility operated by a private entity whose operations affect commerce and fall within at least one of the following categories . . .

- (8) A museum, library, gallery, or other place of public display or collection;
- (9) A park, zoo, amusement park, or other place of recreation."

§ 36.302 Modifications in Policies, Practices, or Procedures

"(a) *General.* A public accommodation shall make reasonable modifications in policies, practices, or procedures, when the modifications are necessary to afford goods, services, facilities, privileges, advantages, or accommodations to individuals with disabilities, unless the public accommodation can demonstrate that making the modifications would fundamentally alter the nature of the goods, services, facilities, privileges, advantages, or accommodations."

Notes

1. Yvonne J. Gist and Lisa I. Hetzel, "We the People: Aging in the United States," Census 2000 Special Report, December 2004, www.census.gov/prod/2004pubs/censr-19.pdf (accessed May 12, 2011).

2. See the U.S. Department of Justice ADA Home Page at www.ada.gov (accessed May 12, 2011).

3. "Facility Information and Handicapped Accessibility," Molly Brown House Museum, www.mollybrown.org/visit-us/accessibility/ (accessed May 11, 2011).

4. See the Molly Brown House Museum website at www.mollybrown.org.

GOOD VISITOR SERVICE, OR "PUT DOWN THE PENCIL AND PUT ON A SMILE!"
Tamara Hemmerlein

Understanding good customer service is not necessarily a given. Some people come by it naturally as a part of their outlook on life. But everyone can learn to be more attentive and training like this should be a part of the professional development of *all* staff.[1]

Most people who work or volunteer in small institutions are familiar with the situation of the doorbell chiming, the phone ringing, or the car driving up just as we hit our stride in writing that newsletter article due tomorrow, come up with the brilliant programming idea that we need to share right away, or start counting the pieces in the bulk-mailing project. My response to those types of interruptions is often a deep sigh while I stop whatever I am doing and get ready to give the next tour or respond to whatever the caller's question may be. Sometimes I catch myself thinking, "Who could possibly have the audacity to interrupt my important museum stuff?" or "Isn't there someone else who could handle this tour?"

It is not always easy to remember that our visitors are one of the most important reasons we exist. But, if you think about it, an institution without visitors is simply a structure, a collection of objects, or piles of papers that someone has to manage. It is the interaction between the visitors and the site that creates meaning and makes our sites relevant. Every once in a while, something happens to remind us of why we do what we do. We sometimes share incredible experiences with our visitors. For instance, there is the little boy who at the end of the tour says, "I've seen three things touched by actual presidents. Me, right here!" Or the person who leaves an art program saying, "Who knew I could sketch something that really looks like something?" Or the repeat visitor who says, "I learn something different every time I come here!" and brings other visitors to the site because it has become a "can't miss" experience.

There are also the moments that confound us or make us want to run screaming from our visitors. For example, there is the visitor who insists on calling the soup tureens in the dining room soup "latrines," despite our best efforts to convince her of the contrary, or the visitor who wants to show that he knows it all and can enlighten everyone, including the museum staff and volunteers.

No matter what job you have in your institution, you will most likely come into contact with visitors of all kinds at some point. As we small museums become more community focused and open to our constituents, we will have to become more fluent in visitor services and interactions. The more we respect our visitors and pay attention to their needs, the better they will support us and see us as vital components in their lives. Good visitor service should never be an afterthought; it should be something that we work to improve every day.

Why Do People Choose to Visit Museums?

Museums are no longer cabinets of curiosity with open doors and displays full of interesting objects; they have become gathering places, sites for discourse, and, in some cases, catalysts for change. Past models of museums as quiet, staid, and exclusive institutions simply do not function in today's world. Visitors come to museums to learn, to interact with the past and with each other, and to have meaningful experiences. To remain relevant, museums increasingly must learn how best to serve their communities.

A great experience begins before visitors even walk through the doors. Anyone who might come into contact with visitors should be trained to provide good visitor service. Ideally museum staff and volunteers think about the basic needs that any individual may have and strive to meet those needs. Everyone has reasons for doing the things they do and making the choices they make. Museum visitors are choosing to spend their time with us, and they are doing that for a variety of very personal reasons. Some, like parents, come so that their children can learn about or be exposed to something that they otherwise would not experience. Visitors come to find out something about themselves in our programs and exhibits. Some come because of the social interaction at the site or within a particular group. All have chosen to visit us, and we should do our best to understand what visitors are expecting from their experience.

Among many theories of why individuals make specific choices, Abraham Maslow's hierarchy of needs is a common one used to understand human motivation. Maslow's original theory was that the needs in each stage must be satisfied for an individual to move to the next stage, beginning with the basic biological and physiological needs (air, food, shelter), moving through needs for safety (security, order, stability), then belongingness and love (social group, family, interaction), then esteem (achievement, mastery, self-esteem), and finishing with self-actualization (fulfillment of personal potential, achievement of personal growth, self-fulfillment). If something changes at any of those stages and the needs are no longer being met, then the individual stops being concerned about the higher-level needs. For example, a visitor who has to use the restroom will not be able to focus on what a guide is saying during a tour. The visitor will fidget and may even become surly until his or her physiological need of using the facilities is met. Judy Rand's "Visitors' Bill of Rights" in *Reinventing the Museum: Historical and Contemporary Perspectives on the Paradigm Shift* is an excellent illustration of the needs of the museum visitor.[2]

To have the best visit possible, visitors need to feel comfortable and safe in the museum space. They need to know how to enter the museum, where to find the amenities, and where they may go once they are inside. They are often looking for a connection with a particular group or idea. Visitors are looking for social experiences with meaningful interactions and self-fulfillment. A museum visit should end with the visitor feeling that his or her needs and expectations have been met. As John Falk, guru of the visitor experience, has noted, "A century ago, only a very few individuals worried about 'self-fulfillment.' . . . Today, self-fulfillment is a driving goal. . . . Self-actualization in one form or another is driving an ever-growing number of individuals."[3] Individuals who choose to visit museums are making that choice from among hundreds of other ways to spend their free time. They want to feel good about the choice and not as though their time and money have been wasted. A visitor who has a bad experience will not return and will not recommend the site to others.

In *The Tipping Point*, Malcolm Gladwell discusses something he calls the "stickiness factor." Stickiness makes something memorable. It has to do with communicating a message in such a way that the message is remembered and can be a catalyst for action or cause some kind of change. Often people try to create stickiness by speaking louder, repeating information, or adding artificial emphasis. But stickiness is not necessarily increased by any of these things. It can be increased in easier and gentler ways.

Museums are increasingly concerned about stickiness, although they do not necessarily use that terminology. Are visitors coming? Do they keep coming back? Do they recommend us to their friends and family? Do they remember the messages that we are trying to convey through our exhibits, tours, and programs? How are we communicating with the visitors? Do we need to shout our messages, or are there better and sometimes quieter ways to reach them?

Good visitor service is an easy and subtle way to ensure your museum's stickiness. When visitors have had a positive experience, they leave a site wanting to discuss what they learned and experienced. They will talk about their visit and encourage people they know to visit also. No one is going to recommend that friends and family visit a site after a miserable experience.

Train Everyone! Even the Janitor!

In many museums, the individuals who work in the "back of the house" are museum professionals: educators, curators, archivists, and the like. They have very specific training for their jobs but often do not receive training in visitor service because they are not generally the first points of contact for visitors. Anyone in your museum who might interact with visitors should receive visitor service

Photo 5.1. *Everyone* should be able to greet visitors with a smile and answer questions about hours of operation, admission costs, and available amenities. (Courtesy of Alison Wright, Lane Place)

training. The training should begin with the basics: assuring that the site is welcoming, that visitors are asked if they need assistance finding their way, and that the site is clean and accessible. As John Falk, along with his colleague Beverly Sheppard, reminds us, "Caring for the cleanliness and convenience of the facilities [and] the clarity of wayfinding aids . . . are direct statements about the institution's attitude toward its visitors; all dramatically influence the likelihood that a visitor will leave feeling positively about the museum, and will choose to return and encourage others to also visit."[4]

As museums work to become more accessible and to connect with the personal experiences of visitors, even those individuals who do not traditionally interact with visitors should learn about good visitor service. For example, the person merely checking on the condition of a displayed artifact might be approached by a visitor and asked about the availability of the public restroom.

In many small institutions, the staff and volunteers who install exhibits, work with collections, and so forth, also function as the frontline staff. Individuals trained for specific jobs within an institution are catapulted into visitor service and should feel prepared to help visitors. Small museum staff and volunteers learn to multitask; their focus can rarely be on just one thing happening at their sites. Projects are in progress, and a visitor needs help in the museum shop. The doorbell or the telephone rings in the middle of a tour, and there is not always a second person on-site to handle the interruption. The seemingly constant interruptions can lead to frustration and annoyance, especially when the staff and volunteers already feel as if they are spread too thin. In *Distracted: The Erosion of Attention and the Coming Dark Age*, Maggie Jackson describes the effects of the multiple demands on our attention: "Nearly a third of workers feel they often do not have time to reflect on or process the work they do. More than half typically have to juggle too many tasks simultaneously and/or are so often interrupted that they find it difficult to get work done."[5]

In spite of any frustration at being interrupted, the staff and volunteers should make the visitor feel welcome and important. Staff and volunteer perceptions of visitors will shape the way visitors are treated. Encourage them to think of the visitors not as interruptions but as opportunities to share information with others. Also encourage staff and volunteers to openly communicate with each other about their experiences with visitors and to talk about what is going well and what needs improvement. Bettering visitor service is an ongoing process and involves dialogue and discussion among staff and volunteers.

Additionally, visitor service training should not be limited to frontline staff only; it should be required for behind-the-scenes museum professionals and volunteers as well. Often training is limited to the particular area in which staff or volunteers work. Museum greeters, shop volunteers, and college interns should be able to answer simple questions with as much confidence and ease as any other staff member. Those individuals are many times the first points of contact for museum visitors and the ones most likely to be seen as accessible and easy to talk to, especially if the visitor thinks that his questions are silly or obvious. Falk and Sheppard describe this common staffing situation: "The most likely place to find 'someone of the people' in today's museum is on the front lines—receptionists, guards, cloak room clerks, sales staff, volunteer docents, gallery teachers, shop and food service staff. These are the individuals most directly dealing with the museum's visitor experience; they are also likely to be the lowest paid and least trained."[6]

Visitor service training should take place with all museum staff and volunteers regardless of time in the institution, staff or volunteer tasks, or physical location within the museum. It is essential for even back-of-house personnel to be able to interact meaningfully with any visitor they might encounter, not just on-site but via e-mail or telephone. Visitors want to be treated with respect and care; they want to feel acknowledged even if they are just asking for the location of the museum shop or directions to the next site they are visiting. Providing all staff and volunteers with effective visitor service training will help to ensure a pleasant experience for everyone, including the staff and volunteers.

How Well Do You Know Your Visitors?

Good visitor service begins with knowing who your visitors are and what they expect from their visits to your institution. You can gather quick-and-dirty demographic information on a sign-in sheet by asking visitors for a home zip code, how many adults and children are in their group, and how they found out about the museum. Another way to gather information is simply to ask staff and volunteers to be more aware of who is visiting and what types of questions they ask. Your frontline staff and volunteers have the most direct contact with visitors and will have a different perspective from those individuals who do not have as much contact with visitors on a daily basis. Encourage communication between frontline and back-of-house staff and volunteers in environments where they feel free to discuss their visitor experiences. Even if your volunteer and staff pool is small, make sharing this information a priority by meeting to discuss observations, posting information for everyone to read, and conducting periodic training.

You might also create a short evaluation form and encourage visitors to fill it out at the end of their visit. Small institutions in the same area might choose to work together to create a value assessment to be given to members

DOS AND DON'TS OF A SUCCESSFUL VISITOR EXPERIENCE

- Do all that you can do to ensure that wayfinding signs are appropriately placed and easy to read. Do not assume that because wayfinding signs are clear to those familiar with your site that they will be clear to visitors.
- Do be sure the exterior of your site is as welcoming as possible. Do not assume that visitors only care about what is on the inside of the museum.
- Do post a sign with your site's hours of operation and admission charges at the entrances to your site. Do not hide this information and expect visitors to come in to ask; many will simply walk away if the information is not there or is unclear.
- Do welcome all visitors, no matter what your position at the museum, with a friendly greeting and smile. Do not ignore visitors even if you are busy with another task or are not normally frontline staff.
- Do offer seating to visitors if necessary. Do not forget to be aware of your visitors and their comfort levels.
- Do make sure that the interior spaces of the museum are clean, especially the restrooms. Do not forget to check the paper towel, soap, and toilet paper dispensers.
- Do have friendly and professional voice mail announcements. Do not record cute or overly long messages.
- Do return calls and e-mail messages promptly. Do not put off responding to inquiries.
- Do be able to direct visitors to the appropriate person or location in response to inquiries. Do not be afraid to admit you do not know something.
- Do be honest with your visitors. Do not promise a visitor something that you or your site cannot provide.
- Do remember to acknowledge visitor questions and concerns. Do not ignore them or belittle the visitor. Visitors generally do not ask unless they truly want to know.
- Do send visitors away from your site with a "Thank you for visiting" and an invitation to come back.

of each institution and distributed throughout the community in order to gather information about the public perception of the sites and how the local community uses them. Compile the findings and share the information with your board, staff, volunteers, members, and the public on your website, in your newsletters, and in press releases to the local media. Publicly communicating the information will let the community and visitors know that you are truly interested in their feedback.

You can also use evaluation cards and value assessments to gather information about your current level of visitor service. Are visitors referring other people to your site? Are they returning and bringing new visitors with them? What would they improve? Remind anyone involved with the institution to listen to what is being said outside of the institution. Constructive eavesdropping at the local grocery store, library, or gathering spot can be a good way to learn about the public view of your institution.

After the information has been gathered and compiled—a great task for an intern or an interested volunteer—use it to create a profile of the typical visitor. As objectively as you can, look at the suggestions for change and improvement that visitors are making. Share the information with your board, staff, and volunteers. Do not be afraid to expose and discuss your museum's visitor service problems. Begin by celebrating the things that are being done right and then move on to criticisms as a way of becoming even better.

For more information on visitor studies and evaluation, please see chapter 2 in this book.

Successful Visitor Service Training

Plan a series of meetings with as many of the staff and volunteers as possible throughout the year. (See textbox 5.5 at the end of this chapter for a sample training outline.) Encourage everyone to become involved in the discussions and use the answers and thoughts to discover the perceptions that the staff and volunteers have of your site and its visitor service. Create an open environment where meaningful interaction can take place. Because you are asking everyone to participate and give honest feedback, be sure to set up ground rules for the interactions that will occur during the meetings. State that everyone will have the opportunity to discuss ideas and that the meetings are not a forum for criticizing other staff and volunteers; rather, they are a way to use visitor, volunteer, and staff feedback and suggestions to improve the institution. The training sessions should be conducted with the same type of respect you would show visitors to the site. In the end, the sessions will be worth the effort expended on them.

HOW ARE WE DOING? A CHECKLIST FOR IMPROVEMENT

- Are frontline staff and volunteers friendly and knowledgeable? What about back-of-house staff and volunteers?
- Has there been training for all staff and volunteers in proper telephone and e-mail etiquette?
- Do the staff and volunteers know each other and know to whom to refer visitor inquiries?
- Are the staff and volunteers easily identified by visitors?
- Do the staff and volunteers receive training on handling difficult and emergency visitor situations?
- Are all staff and volunteers, regardless of job, given visitor services training?
- Are the staff and volunteers offered opportunities to go on field trips to other sites to gather information and learn about visitor service in other organizations, including nonmuseum institutions? Are post mortems of the trips conducted?
- Is information about current exhibits, frequently asked questions, and tips for good visitor service placed in staff and volunteer spaces?
- Are staff and volunteers encouraged to discuss their visitor service experiences and to aid each other in finding solutions to difficult issues?

Think about interactions from both museum and visitor perspectives. Ask for participants to share experiences they have had with visitors both inside and outside the institution. Talk about what did and did not go well. Encourage honesty without cruelty; talk about interactions, but do not mock visitors. Everyone needs to vent; we have all had difficult or odd visitors and days when we do not really want to answer any more questions. Assure your staff and volunteers that it is okay to share their frustrations and stressful situations. Venting can lead to new ideas and solutions, but what is said should be kept confidential and as respectful as possible.

Quality training sessions can be lengthy and mentally exhausting, but they should also be opportunities for growth and social interaction. Emphasize that the things the staff and volunteers learn can be used outside of their jobs and in their personal lives. It is important for the training sessions to be in comfortable and relaxed settings. Your staff and volunteers should receive the same type of consideration as your visitors. They will not be able to focus on learning if they feel uncomfortable or insecure. Providing tasty snacks can be both a mild incentive to come and a way to help make the environment more comfortable.

Training Is Not Orientation

Do not expect to be able to train your volunteers and staff all at once, and do not treat training in the same way that you would orientation. Orientation is generally a one-time or annual experience for volunteers and staff. Training is ongoing and should be viewed as part of a continuing education process for staff and volunteers. Be clear that the training is important and should be taken seriously, but also that it should be interesting and fun.

The next several sections describe topics or methods to consider. Each section could be the subject of an individual training session if you meet frequently, or they could be combined for lengthier sessions.

Set the Stage

Start the initial visitor service training with questions for the staff and volunteers. The questions should set the stage for all the training sessions and help the participants focus on the purpose of the training. You can also use the answers and any discussion that results from the questions to set some goals for the training. You might find that the goals you had in mind do not dovetail with the perceptions of the participants. Work with your staff and volunteers to make sure that you are all on the same page about visitors and their needs.

Find out what the participants' perceptions of your site and visitors are by asking simple questions. You might want to consider the following questions, among others, during this meeting:

- Who are your visitors?
- Why are they visiting your site?
- What is the public perception of your site?
- What are the visitor expectations of your site?
- How would a "mystery visitor" (someone visiting undercover) evaluate your site?
- Would you visit your site if you did not work or volunteer there? Why or why not?
- What would be the absolute perfect visitor experience at your site? How does the normal visitor experience compare to the perfect visit?
- What are three strengths and three weaknesses of visitor services at your site? Evaluate your strengths; why are you better at those things

than others? Think of strategies to improve the weaknesses; can you use some of the same strategies that you used to create your strengths?

- What can you change to provide good visitor services?
- What cannot be changed? If something cannot be changed, how can it be used in its current form or tweaked a bit to provide better visitor service?

First Impressions

Include a tour of the site inside and out. Only focusing on the interior of the site can mean that problems outside are overlooked. The exterior will give your visitor his or her first impression of the site. A clean and welcoming exterior starts the visit on a positive note. Try to start from the very first location that visitors see—the parking lot, the surrounding street, the sidewalk—and approach the site as if you were seeing it for the first time instead of the hundredth. Check for cracking walkways, unruly landscaping, trash—anything that could give a visitor a negative impression of the site before he or she even enters.

Be sure to pay particular attention to signs and obstacles to visitor comfort. Look at the handicapped-accessible parking spaces and entrances. Are they as well maintained and welcoming as the other entrances? If they are not, what message you are sending to disabled visitors, their friends, and their families? Ask staff and volunteers what they see, and be open to both positive and negative comments. If there are problems, ask for solutions and ideas for improvement. Celebrate what you do well and create ways to improve on those things that you are not doing well.

Learning the Basics

Everyone should learn the basics: greeting on-site visitors, answering phones, e-mail messages, responding to all types of visitor questions, and giving warm visitor send-offs. When staff or volunteers answer the phone, they should identify the institution and themselves and offer to be of service. A simple "John Smith Museum, this is Jane, how I may I help you?" is all that is needed. The same sort of rule should be followed when responding to an e-mail message. Give the appropriate salutation and thanks—"Dear Mr. Jones, thank you for your interest in the John Smith Museum"—and close with an offer to answer any further questions, your name, title, and contact information.

Each time an exhibit changes or a program is added or updated, staff and volunteers should receive additional training so that they can better answer any questions. Everyone at the site should understand the exhibit, its goals, and any programs planned in conjunction with it. A schedule of events should be available to all staff and volunteers. Keep a copy by the phone and in the reception area as a quick reference. Include visitor service training in any staff or volunteer meetings you may have—even museums with very small staffs or a group of core volunteers should be discussing updates and changes in the museum on a regular basis.

Emphasize that visitors and their comfort are very important to a successful institution and that excellent visitor service is something everyone involved with your site should strive to achieve. Ask people to share great customer service examples from nonmuseum situations (like McDonalds or the DMV) and discuss how they can apply to your situation. Provide each volunteer and staff member with a procedural booklet including examples of any forms they might encounter and basic institutional information such as hours of operations, admission charges, facility use policies, organizational structure, emergency reporting procedures, and so forth. Include brief job descriptions of each position so that everyone knows who does what and to whom to refer visitor inquiries if necessary. Keep a copy in the reception and break areas if you have the space. Place a reminder in your calendar to update the materials on a monthly or quarterly basis.

Do Not Judge a Book by Its Cover

Visitors come in all colors, shapes, and sizes. While we may have some general expectations about the types of visitors at our sites, we cannot expect every visitor to fit within a preconceived idea or demographic. In relaying an example of stellar customer service and success, Malcolm Gladwell points to the case of a New Jersey car salesman who sells nearly twice the number of cars each month as the average salesperson. The successful salesman works to avoid snap judgments based on appearance and tries to treat each customer in the same way. Each of your visitors is an individual. Do not assume that the teenage girl is not interested in an exhibit on local industry or that the older man is not interested in the current technology exhibit. The visitor who is texting may not be ignoring the guide but telling friends about the museum and encouraging them to visit. Be sure to look beyond your visitors' exterior and pay attention to their responses and actions. You will be able to give them a much better and more personal experience.

That is not to say that we should view our visitors as a monolithic block or that each visitor is looking for exactly the same experience at our sites. But it is important to remember that appearances are not necessarily indicative of a specific visitor or group of visitors' needs or interaction desires. Share your own experiences of a surprising visitor, and ask others to share theirs. Ask people to think about family and friends who do not fit the mold suggested by their appearance. Remind the group that the basics of good visitor service are the same for every interaction.

Role Playing

We will all have some type of negative experience at our sites at some point. If your staff and volunteers are comfortable with role playing, have them alternate playing the roles of less-than-perfect visitors and frontline staff. Staff and volunteers will be challenged by visitors on occasion. Give them some scenarios of challenging experiences that they might encounter as they interact with visitors and ask them to work through the scenarios (see textbox 5.3).

Let them struggle with the situations a bit and try to find a good solution as a group. After the role playing, ask other members what they might have done in the same situation. Be sure to have your own successful strategies in mind in case your group is stymied by the situation (see textbox 5.4).

Thanking Your Visitors

During the training, remind participants that it is important to remember to thank visitors at the end of any interaction they may have with them.

Photo 5.2. Remember to thank visitors for spending time at your site and invite them back again! (Courtesy of Kara Edie, General Lew Wallace Study & Museum)

PROBLEMATIC VISITOR SCENARIOS

(Remember these scenarios can and should be adapted to fit your needs and experiences.)

1. A visitor walks up to the front door of the museum and complains that he has been unable to figure out which door is the main entrance. He has walked around the building several times and finally decided to come to the front door and ring the bell. He states that it is a difficult place to get into. How do you respond?
2. On a day that the museum is normally closed to visitors, two staff members notice a tour bus pulling up on the street alongside the museum. There is no tour on the schedule, and a quick check with the local visitors and convention bureau comes up negative for a tour as well. About forty-five people disembark and walk to the front door. The doorbell rings, and the tour operator announces that the group is there for a guided tour. What do you do?
3. A family of four comes to your site for a visit. One of the children is an infant, and during the visit, one of the adults asks where the nearest bathroom with a changing station is. The problem is that your site has one very small restroom with no changing facilities. What do you say to the visitor?
4. A visitor comes into the museum, and the docent notices that he has an oddly shaped horn wrapped around his arm. During the tour the visitor asks if he can sing some songs that he has written and, at the end of the tour, asks if he can blow his horn from the front porch of the museum. How should the docent handle the situation?
5. A visitor to the museum receives a phone call on her cell. She answers and gradually begins to speak louder and louder. You notice that other visitors are becoming annoyed by the commotion caused by her conversation. What action, if any, do you take?
6. During a tour, some visitors are very knowledgeable and seem to be challenging the tour guide. Feeling heckled, the tour is getting tense while other visitors are becoming uncomfortable with the situation. How can the tour guide diffuse the tension and keep going with the tour?
7. A visitor is touching everything that interests her, in spite of written signs and consistent verbal reminders. How do you stop the insistent visitor?

POTENTIAL SUCCESSFUL SCENARIO OUTCOMES

1. Welcome the visitor and apologize for the difficulty. Do not be insulted. Be positive and listen. The visitor will calm down, and the visit will get back on the right track. If it is appropriate before the tour, ask how the signage, approach, or entry might be improved to make it easier for the visitor to know where the main entrance is. If it is not appropriate at the beginning of the tour, ask at the end. Thank the visitor for being willing to give feedback and helping to make future visits better. Remember, we see our sites almost every day and take for granted where the entrances are.

2. Stop what you are doing and give yourself a minute to be surprised and gather your thoughts, whatever they may be. Then open the door, welcome the visitors, and give a tour as usual. Turning away a full busload of visitors will not lead to anything positive for your institution. It is likely not the visitors' fault that there was a communications breakdown along the line somewhere. They should not be made to feel uncomfortable; their tour should still be a great experience. As the visitors are boarding the bus to leave, take the time to talk to the person in charge of the group and ask for contact information for his or her organization. Explain that you are simply going to pass the information along to the appropriate staff person at your institution so that the process for scheduling tours can be clarified. Do not be confrontational or lay blame. The person with the group might not be the one in charge of making arrangements, and confrontation will not solve anything.

3. Show your visitor the bathroom, and see if he or she is comfortable using it. If there is no way for the visitor to use the bathroom to change a diaper, then offer the visitor the use of another area, even if that area is not usually open for the public. Be willing to offer space in a break room or an office. A miserable child will cause the adults to be miserable, and the visit will be ruined. You can always clean a desk, table, or floor; you cannot always win back an angry parent.

4. Do not stare at the horn, and do not make assumptions about the visitor. You might want to ask the visitor about the horn from the start and ask him to check it at the front desk. Assure him that it

(*continued*)

will be there for him when the tour is done. If he does not want to check the horn, then ask him to please make sure that he is careful as you go through the museum. When he asks to sing or to play his horn, respond in a way that is comfortable for you and not dismissive of the visitor. If you do not mind listening, an option is to ask him to wait until he has exited the museum to perform. Listen briefly, thank him for coming, and tell him to have a nice day. If you are uncomfortable, thank him for the offer, but suggest that the museum is not really the best place for him to perform.

5. At the beginning of the tour, politely ask the visitors to silence their electronic devices so that everyone can enjoy the tour. Hopefully, this will avoid the issue altogether. Once the tour has been interrupted by the phone call, simply ask the visitor to move to another area of the institution. Suggest the entryway, a hallway, or even a porch. Be sure that you are not sending the visitor to an area that will cause problems for another group. Your fellow staff and volunteers will not thank you for passing the problem on to them.

6. The docent should not confront the visitor or heckle in return. Visitors do not come to museums to engage in confrontations with the staff. Try not to get angry or be insulted. Often the visitor simply wants to be acknowledged in some way. Comment on his interest and encourage other visitors to share their knowledge as well. Allow time and space for meaningful interaction; do not shut it down. You might learn something from the visitor. The interaction could yield new information. It also might result in a change in the way you phrase information during the tour if the visitor comments point out confusing wording or statements. This tour and future tours will benefit from increased knowledge.

7. Tell your staff and volunteers that it is okay to be firm with the artifact handler—it is their job to help protect the artifacts—while remembering to be respectful of the visitor. Model good behavior for the visitors by not touching the artifacts or leaning and sitting on furniture. Sometimes white gloves can be used as an effective way to illustrate the importance of not handling the artifacts. If it is part of the tour for docents to hold or pick something up, have them use gloves and explain why they are using them.

Acknowledge the time and effort that visitors spent to contact you or to come to your site. Recognize their importance to what you do. Stop whatever you are doing to acknowledge the visitors, even if you are not the person with whom they had the most interaction. A simple "Thank you for visiting!" from anyone at the museum is often the icing on the cake of a great visitor experience. Do not forget to invite the visitors to come back again and to bring friends with them.

Ending the Training Session

At the end of each training session, remember also to thank the staff and volunteers for their time and attention. Model good visitor service by treating the staff and volunteers in the same way you would like them to treat visitors. After training sessions, provide follow-up. If concerns were raised, explain how they were addressed. Include ongoing training for staff and volunteers.

Good Visitor Services As a Way of Life

Ultimately, good visitor services should become intuitive and automatic, but you always want to create a supportive climate. Create visitor service awards. Include positive visitor service stories in both in-house and outside communications like newsletters and websites. Encourage continued sharing among staff and volunteers of positive and negative experiences. Be sure to include the ways in which less than positive situations were handled and problems were solved. Keep the lines of communication open and respond promptly to visitor service concerns.

Providing visitors with a great experience at your site is one of the easiest and most effective ways to increase visitation, improve public awareness, and assure the continued success of your institution. Effective visitor service leads to a more positive atmosphere within the institution and more buzz outside.

TEXTBOX 5.5

SAMPLE VISITOR SERVICE TRAINING OUTLINE

(Be sure to structure your training sessions to fit your institution and its needs.)

I. Welcome and introductions
II. Training ground rules
   a. Be respectful and listen to others.
   b. Everyone has an opportunity to speak, but no one is required to speak.
   c. There are no stupid comments or questions.
   d. Provide other institution guidelines as needed.
III. Training goals and objectives (institution specific): What is good visitor service?
   a. List three strengths and three weaknesses of visitor services at your site. Evaluate your strengths; why are you better at those things than others? Think of strategies to improve the weaknesses; can you use some of the same strategies that you used to create your strengths?
   b. What can you change to provide better visitor services?
   c. What cannot be changed? If something cannot be changed, how can it be used in its current form or tweaked a bit to provide better visitor service?
IV. Visitor information
   a. Why are visitors important?
   b. Consider staff and volunteer perceptions of visitors.
      1. Who are your visitors?
      2. Why are they visiting your site?
      3. What are visitors' expectations/perceptions of your site?
   c. Summarize visitor surveys or assessments.
V. Visitor, volunteer, and staff perceptions of site
   a. What are your perceptions of your site?
   b. How would a "mystery visitor" (someone visiting undercover) evaluate your site?
   c. Would you visit your site if you did not work or volunteer there? Why or why not?
   d. What are some of the positive and negative visitor service experiences you have had?

       1. At other institutions

       2. At nonmuseum institutions

    e. What would be the perfect visitor experience at your site? How does the normal visitor experience compare to the perfect visit?

 VI. Exterior and interior site tour and evaluation

    a. Are the grounds and exterior clean, well kept, and welcoming?

    b. Is there adequate signage?

    c. Are the accessible areas clean and easy to navigate?

    d. Are the bathrooms clean and well stocked?

    e. Is there adequate seating for visitors?

    f. Consider other site-specific questions.

VII. Visitor service basics

    a. Greeting and thanking visitors

    b. Answering visitor questions (on-site)

    c. Knowing about amenities and exhibits

    d. Answering the phone

    e. Responding to written communications, including e-mail messages

    f. Responding to visitor inquiries about the local area

    g. Considering site-specific basics

VIII. Role playing

 IX. Questions, answers, and venting

  X. Training summary and further training opportunities

Resources

Anderson, Gail, ed. *Reinventing the Museum: Historical and Contemporary Perspectives on the Paradigm Shift.* Lanham, MD: AltaMira Press, 2004.

Falk, John H. *Identity and the Museum Visitor Experience.* Walnut Creek, CA: Left Coast Press, Inc., 2009.

Falk, John H., and Beverly K. Sheppard. *Thriving in the Knowledge Age: New Business Models for Museums and Other Cultural Institutions.* Lanham, MD: AltaMira Press, 2006.

Levin, Amy K., ed. *Defining Memory: Local Museums and the Construction of History in America's Changing Communities.* Lanham, MD: AltaMira Press, 2007.

Rosenzwieg, Roy, and David Thelen. *The Presence of the Past: Popular Uses of History in American Life.* New York: Columbia University Press, 2000.

Weil, Stephen E. *Making Museums Matter.* Washington, DC: Smithsonian Books, 2002.

Resources may also be accessed online by using the following search terms:

- Customer service
- Customer service manuals
- How-to customer service
- How-to visitor service
- Visitor service
- Visitor service manuals

Notes

1. John Falk and Beverly Sheppard, *Thriving in the Knowledge Age* (Lanham, MD: AltaMira Press, 2006), 114.

2. Judy Rand, "Visitors' Bill of Rights," in *Reinventing the Museum: Historical and Contemporary Perspectives on the Paradigm Shift* (Lanham, MD: AltaMira Press, 2004), 158–59.

3. Falk and Sheppard, *Thriving*, 55.

4. Falk and Sheppard, *Thriving*, 115.

5. Maggie Jackson, *Distracted: The Erosion of Attention and the Coming Dark Age* (Amherst, MA: Prometheus Books, 2008), 17.

6. Falk and Sheppard, *Thriving*, 114.

CHAPTER SIX
NEW ROLES FOR SMALL MUSEUMS
Candace Tangorra Matelic

How can your small museum determine if it is making a meaningful difference in its community? This chapter focuses on why and how small museums are transforming to address what matters in their communities and, in doing so, how they are becoming more relevant and sustainable organizations. For many organizations, this has become a matter of survival. New roles for small museums emerge through honestly engaging the community, discovering what the community cares about, working with other organizations to address community needs, and rediscovering the spirit or passions that uniquely define each individual small museum.

Why Should Small Museums Change?

For decades the museum field has pushed and helped small museums to "do everything right," or to operate according to accepted professional standards. The to-do list has been long, and at times overwhelming, as it has included proper care of collections, preservation of historic buildings, reliance on up-to-date scholarship, development of exciting exhibits and interesting interpretive programs, strong management and fiscal policies, responsible governance, and active fund and friend raising. Now the field has entered an era in which it is more important to "do the right things" by demonstrating that museums, historic sites, and cultural organizations matter to their communities. The traditional activities of collecting, preserving, researching, exhibiting, and interpreting are simply no longer adequate.

Three significant paradigm shifts, or transformations in our thinking, in the museum field now guide the measurement of the public value of our organizations:

Mandating public service: As Stephen Weil, Harold Skramstad, and many other luminaries in our field have advocated, this is the most recent significant shift in focus and priority for museums, historic sites, and cultural organizations. The central purpose of museums is to serve their many publics at the level of making a meaningful difference in the lives of individuals and contributing significantly to the communities they serve. This mandate means that these organizations must demonstrate their public value and positive social outcome and declare these in mission statements and program descriptions for all activities. Weil powerfully expressed this mandate in 2002 in an article titled "Transformed from a Cemetery of Bric-a-Brac":

> Common virtually everywhere today is the conviction that public service is central to what a museum is all about. How that is expressed may differ from one country to another, but almost nowhere is there anybody now left who still believes that the museum is its own excuse for being.

For most museums, this mandate is about reframing their organizational models to focus on long-term effectiveness rather than short-term efficiency. It is a new way of thinking, a new perspective for planning, budgeting, and organizational assessment. Often, the most difficult transition is toward understanding that the inherent worth of collections and sites is necessary but not sufficient to demonstrate public value. These things matter only if the organization matters.

Making interpretation, programs, and community engagement everyone's business: A second paradigm shift is the understanding that everyone in the organization, from the board to curatorial staff to the frontline staff and volunteers, is responsible for the public dimension of the museum, or for interpretation, public programs, outreach, and community engagement. These components of a museum's operation must be organizational priorities rather than delegated to whoever is responsible for programs. A useful interpretive framework—one that puts stories into the context of universal concepts and ideas—provides guidance for research, collections, marketing, and fundraising, as well as public programs, exhibits, publications, events, and other methods of communicating to audiences. Museums of all sizes and focuses can utilize interpretation as a powerful way to engage people and facilitate timely dialogue and deep reflection about important issues because people come to museums to learn about people—their lives, values, trials and tribulations, joys, and contributions. They come to reflect on their own lives, and the lives of their families, friends, neighbors, and business associates. They come to get a new perspective, a new understanding of other people, places, and times, and to be renewed, reinvigorated, and even inspired. By making interpretation, programs, and community engagement everyone's responsibility, museums can become "dialogic places," as described by Stan Carbone, director of the Jewish Heritage Centre of Western Canada. To embrace this shift, many museums must transform their internal values and organizational cultures to embrace leadership at all levels; redefine the roles of professional staff; empower all staff, volunteers, and the community to participate in planning and decision-making; utilize teamwork with community involvement; and integrate ongoing visitor studies into their operations.

Becoming learning organizations: This third shift is about "walking the talk," or valuing learning for stakeholders, including those people who have an existing relationship with the museum, such as staff, board members, and volunteers, as well as visitors. It is about understanding the inherent difficulty and complexity of organizational change and touching hearts and minds before expecting any transformation to occur. Learning organizations use their knowledge and experience to become more effective by going beyond the status quo to grow and evolve. If an organization has embraced this concept, then the criteria for making organizational decisions and setting priorities include learning outcomes as well as short-term performance and the bottom line. The organization values innovation, experimentation, flexibility, and initiative. Knowledge is openly shared, and everyone is encouraged to apply it to problem solving. Leaders at all levels use systems thinking to improve the organization as an integrated ensemble, establish relationships with external groups and organizations, and build long-term sustainability. For museums, historic sites, and cultural organizations to move toward becoming learning organizations, they must learn to value people as their most critical resource and help them develop their knowledge and skills. They must also understand that organizational development means much more than building new facilities and getting more money. It entails learning about effective teamwork and designing new operational structures that focus on long-term effectiveness as well as short-term efficiency. Organizational development includes deepening relationships and collaboration with other community organizations through meaningful work and envisioning the museum's future as a highly valued community player.

These new directions represent enormous shifts in thinking about museums, sites, and cultural organizations, with different underlying values, and for some colleagues and stakeholders, they are downright scary, in part because they challenge traditional professional standards, roles, and practices. Also, it is difficult to predict exactly where an organization will end up once this transformation process is under way. For some people and risk-aversive organizations, this uncertainty is very disconcerting. It requires a leap of faith. However, once it is embraced, and the journey begun with openness and sincerity, these new directions and roles can be exciting, rewarding, and even liberating because they move our organizations closer to a path of broad community support.

So, how do small museums, historic sites, and cultural organizations begin this journey of discovery and transformation? The easiest way to start is to undertake a process of community engagement. It may require some organizational development to get stakeholders on board, or at least willing to go along to see what happens. The following discussion provides some practical steps for engaging community, along with a deeper exploration of who constitutes community, what engagement is and is not, and why engagement can change how the museum sets goals and operates.

How Do We Define Community?

There are many ways to define what forms a community, including shared interests and experiences, common affiliations, demographics, and geographic location. While it is fine to build networks of stakeholders, including members, volunteers, reenactors, and past participants in your organization's programs, I am defining community as the people who live in the geographic area of your museum. Depending on the scope of your organization's mission, this geographic community could be local, regional, state, provincial, or national. For our purposes, it is more useful to think in terms of geography than in terms of stakeholders and affiliations. This geographic definition of community is important because the place where your organization does business is your foundation—your organization is a member of this community, regardless of how active it has been in civic affairs, and the people who live in your community are your organization's constituents. Your geographic community provides resources for your organization, such as supplies, equipment, marketing, knowledge, and expertise. As your organization becomes a more active contributor to community life, these resources grow. Also, every geographic community has a distinguishing character and spirit that emerges over time from its people and history. This means that community engagement and service are different in every community. Each cultural organization must forge its own way. Yet another way to think about community engagement is pushing beyond your organization's existing stakeholders and friends.

Table 6.1. What Community Engagement IS and IS NOT

Community Engagement IS:	Community Engagement IS NOT:
Identifying and addressing what the community cares about.	Identifying what the community can do for your organization.
Doing things that really matter (e.g., activities focused on building better communities).	Token exhibits and programs about or with community groups.
Establishing long-term relationships and partnerships with other community groups.	Occasional stakeholder input meetings or an annual visitor survey.
Working with community groups to plan and offer your programs and activities, and sharing the control, acknowledgement, and proceeds.	Continuing to control and run your programs and activities, yet expecting other community organizations to participate and donate.
Getting involved in community activities outside of your organization.	Expecting reciprocity for contributions to the community outside of your organization.

What Is Community Engagement?

Community engagement involves identifying and addressing what people care about and doing things that really matter—for example, conducting activities focused on building better communities. It entails identifying and establishing long-term relationships and partnerships with other community groups and going beyond the traditional alliances with other cultural or educational organizations. The engagement must first focus on the whole community. This is part of the process of building trust, learning about enduring needs and issues, and seeking new connections by discovering shared visions, often with the most unlikely groups and community organizations. The focus can and will come back to your organization, and it will be much more productive if you begin with the larger focus of building a better community.

It is also important to understand what community engagement is not. It is not simply occasional stakeholder-input meetings, an annual visitor survey, or token exhibits and programs about or with community groups. In fact, sometimes this approach is worse than doing nothing as it raises expectations of meaningful involvement without the follow-through. Community engagement is also not simply about identifying what the community can do for your organization. This second point may sound counterintuitive, but if the community perceives that the engagement process is solely about your organization, some people will decline to participate because they do not feel that they have any connection with or expertise about your organization. Also, they may tell you what they think you want to hear instead of offering creative ideas and solutions that address broader, shared challenges.

Inspiring Examples with Different Starting Points

Before considering my guidelines and steps in the engagement process, let us explore how five very diverse history organizations, at varying points in their existence and development, used community engagement as a catalyst to start changing their organizations. They used the input of community to move toward fundamentally different ways of doing business. These examples demonstrate how each museum's community helped it articulate a new organizational identity and shape a new, more fulfilling future. I hope that you and your organization will have the courage to begin the engagement process after reading about how other organizations have made this journey.

Amherst Historical Society, Amherst, Massachusetts

A highly educated and culturally aware populace distinguishes the charming New England community of Amherst, which has five colleges nearby, a

145

Photo 6.1. As the kickoff for a strategic planning process, the Amherst Historical Society worked with their community to envision a new future for their organization. They started by articulating what Amherst most deeply cared about. (Courtesy of the Amherst Historical Society)

rich agricultural and literary past, and a strong spirit of independence and social justice. Like so many small historical societies across North America, the Amherst Historical Society (AHS) is headquartered in one of the oldest houses in town, located on a central downtown street, adjacent to the library. The building requires ongoing restoration and upkeep, yet offers small exhibit and program spaces that are only available during the seasons when heat is not required, since the house is not modernized except for a few areas. The organization offered a number of annual programs and had a few successful publications, such as the popular history book *Amherst A to Z: Amherst, Mass., 1759–2009*. However, with a part-time director, volunteers, and dwindling financial resources, the society's board faced the challenge of transforming itself so that it could survive. The organization realized that its future depended on a better relationship with the community.

The Amherst Historical Society began its community engagement process with a training session for the board to help its members understand the ways they might transform their operations in response to changing paradigms in the field. Out of the first gathering came the strong sense that AHS should set up a community working group to work with stakeholders throughout the planning process. Everyone agreed that the next steps should include articulating a new organizational vision and a set of strategic directions.

The strategy that emerged from the community engagement process included building and diversifying the board, working with community partners for all future programs, using the entire community for events and activities, reaching out to all residents, including people who were not active in civic affairs, and conceptually developing the historic house as a headquarters and community center rather than a historic house museum. The AHS board acted quickly to build its membership, and this transformative step alone brought new energy, ideas, and resources to the organization. During a second gathering, community representatives worked with AHS stakeholders to continue the planning process. They outlined the necessary steps to move toward implementing the strategic directions and explored a number of possible scenarios for the historic house. Following the second gathering, the society formed a long-range planning committee that continues to explore options for transforming the headquarters into a more useable facility, working with the neighboring library and other community organizations.

This example demonstrates how a small historical society can use community engagement to reconnect with its community and gather valuable ideas and support about its future, reinvigorate its board, and reinvent itself after nearly a century of operation.

Galt Museum and Archives, Lethbridge, Alberta

This museum in southwestern Alberta, Canada, took a new approach to engaging its community through its exhibits. In the fall of 2009, in preparation for a "Treasures and Curiosities" exhibit on display from February through May 2010, the museum invited one hundred community members (including business leaders, government representatives, and the mayor), along with staff and board members, to choose their two favorite artifacts from the collection to be included in the exhibit. Intentionally eclectic, the exhibit drew on the broad content scope of the museum's collections, covering (as described in the press release for exhibit participation) "commerce, immigration, education, community services, religion, transportation, military service, diversity, and the personal lives of individuals who chose to live here." The Galt advertised the wide variety of objects in the collection as well as the "curiosities" it held.

The process went like this: The Galt Museum staff trained a group of twelve volunteers to help the community members choose a subject area and period and then to pick objects by looking together through the collections database and storage areas. If an object sounded interesting, they would go and look at it. The community participants were often very moved by the memories related to the objects they saw, and some people took a number of hours to decide on their objects. The preparation process created a buzz of anticipation in the community about the museum and the exhibit.

The "Treasures and Curiosities" exhibit included the participants' personal stories about why they chose the particular object, and as one visitor noted, this approach "added interest and depth" to the exhibit. Another visitor commented, "The stories and histories provided by the community members made the pieces relevant and interesting, beyond the mere value of the object." The exhibit was designed to look like crates and storage, with labels looking like tags.

This example demonstrates that small museums have many tools to utilize in engaging their communities, not the least of which is their collections. Director Susan Burrows-Johnson commented, "The successful engagement of the community in 'what is in the collection' was a reminder about the use of objects and about community participation. The time, commitment, and emotional response from our community members to the objects was the most extraordinary part of the process." Following the well-attended exhibit, the community viewed the museum in a new light and, of course, has asked for another exhibit of this kind in the future.

Historic Germantown Preserved, Germantown, Pennsylvania

In the Northwest Philadelphia neighborhood of Germantown, a group of fifteen (originally thirteen) historic sites formed a consortium, Historic Germantown Preserved (HGP), to work together rather than compete with one another. The HGP undertook a community engagement process in 2007 and 2008, supported by the Heritage Philadelphia Program of the Pew Center for Arts & Heritage, to streamline and share strategies for organizational development, marketing, and interpretive planning. The yearlong process included initial conversations with groups of community representatives, including many people from the neighborhood who had not had meaningful interaction with the sites and the HGP, to get acquainted and identify a series of community issues. One memorable session gathered fifty people who worked in small groups brainstorming collaborative programs; the event was capped with an ice cream social. Throughout the project, stakeholders from all the sites met on a regular basis to stay up to date on the activities. A team of consultants, with expertise in interpretive planning, organizational development, and marketing, and a team of scholars advised HGP stakeholders. An important outcome of the community engagement process was that the HGP sites agreed on four key concepts as a common content framework for daily interpretation at the individual sites, as well as collaborative programs and events. This is quite an accomplishment. The framework helped to shape a new marketing plan and brand: "Freedom's Backyard." The process was the catalyst for several major steps forward in the HGP's organizational development: HGP organizations jointly supported a program coordinator who worked out of a centralized office in the Germantown Historical Society.

This transformative initiative continued to bear fruit following the initial community-engagement process. For example, the HGP received subsequent Pew funding for "Germantown Works," a series of programs about twentieth-century Germantown history, building on one of the four interpretive concepts in the interpretive framework: "Hard Work: An Industrious People Creating Commerce and Culture." As described by HGP program coordinator Anne Burnett, these programs had input from leading scholar and neighborhood stakeholders:

> Offered in partnership with Germantown Speaks, a related grant initiative by the local Neighborhood Interfaith Movement, the public forums and programs served the dual purposes of training local high school students in oral history interviewing, recording, and photography, while engaging area seniors, church members and elected officials in sharing their stories through lively, moving intergenerational dialogue. Video and audio capture of these personal histories of 20th century Germantown allowed for continued sharing and discussion via HGP's Freedom's Backyard website. This project enriched the delivery of interpretive content and extended the reach of HGP sites, and built sustainable relationships with new community partners.

Organizationally, the 2007–2008 interpretive plan and subsequent Germantown Works project laid important groundwork for capacity building, attracting the support of a local foundation for development of a business plan to hire an executive director and support staff, which furthered the HGP's ability to promote and serve its fifteen historic sites and the Northwest Philadelphia community as a whole.

South Dakota Agricultural Heritage Museum, Brookings, South Dakota

This small museum is located on the campus of South Dakota State University (SDSU) in a building that once served as an agricultural stockyard, establishing its historic connection to SDSU as a land grant university in a state where agriculture is a leading enterprise. As a museum facility, the space is woefully substandard. It has one large room for exhibits plus a smaller adjacent space that supports changing exhibits and programs, as well as a tiny shop. The basement houses staff offices and collection storage for smaller items, while larger objects are stored in a separate building. Director Mac Harris was hired with a mandate for change, and finding a new home for the museum was a big part of his charge. He established a new board with representatives from across the state and began to use community engagement to define a new vision and future for the museum. It was clear that the museum should play a more central role in the life of SDSU and do more to fulfill its mandate as the state agricultural museum.

The museum began its strategic planning process in the fall of 2008 with an audience and community study, to learn more about current visitors, museum members, and the community at large, including the university community. The museum initiated a series of conversations with faculty, students, local teachers, and community leaders about the distinctiveness of South Dakota as a place, the state's important agricultural past and future, the special characteristics of South Dakotans, and how the museum could better serve its various audiences. The museum discovered that its primary audience should be the university community, followed by a statewide audience and traditional museum audiences, such as school groups. Wanting the museum to be more integrated into academic life, faculty and students suggested that interdisciplinary teams comprising individuals from each group work with the museum to develop exhibits for display all over campus—in effect, considering the entire campus a museum. They also discussed the development of an interdisciplinary curriculum titled "Agriculture in American Life." Their input shaped the vision for an innovative new facility that would include learning laboratories, classrooms, indoor and outdoor exhibits, space for large events and conferences with alumni and leading agricultural thinkers, open storage for collections (including collections from a number of other academic departments), and a green facility that could be utilized as a teaching tool.

Since the initial dialogues with the university community, the museum has continued the engagement process and broadened the scope to include additional departments, representatives of agricultural commodity groups, and agricultural extension across the state. As of this writing, a feasibility study for a new facility is under way, and the museum is seeking funding to engage citizens across the state about how to better serve them and address current and future agricultural issues. In sum, the South Dakota Agricultural Heritage Museum is in a very different place from where it would be if it had conducted a more traditional, internally focused strategic planning process. The community engagement led the organization to deepen relationships with other university departments, envision a learning center rather than a traditional museum for its new headquarters, and reframe its future purpose and operations.

The Mill at Anselma, Chester Springs, Pennsylvania

This historic site utilized community engagement early in its organizational history as it transitioned from a preservation project to a historic site open to the public. Four years after the board was formed in 1998, it completed an initial master plan, hired its first professional director, Heather Reiffer, and opened to the public with regular hours. By 2004, it had restored the mill's equipment to operating condition. The following year, it started to restore the other five

Photo 6.2. Results from the initial community gathering were promising enough to encourage the Mill at Anselma board to form a community working group. These community representatives participated in the mill's strategic interpretation and program planning process during the following year. (Courtesy of Candace T. Matelic)

structures on the site and opened a visitor center in a barn. The site was named a National Historic Landmark in April 2005 because it is a rare example of a small, custom, water-powered gristmill with surviving, completely intact equipment that predates Oliver Evans's mill technology—Evans revolutionized flour milling at the close of the eighteenth century with the development of continuous-process production.

The mill's community engagement process began in 2003 with a preliminary session for the board to learn about the current thinking in the field and the benefits of community involvement. Following this session, the board shifted to focus on site interpretation and visitor amenities and held an initial community workshop. The results were so promising that it formed a community working group to participate in subsequent planning. In 2004 the mill secured support from the Heritage Philadelphia Program of the Pew Center for Arts & Heritage for a comprehensive and strategic interpretative and program planning process that occurred in 2004 and 2005. Scholars, mill stakeholders, interpretive planning consultants (audience advocates and a coordinating team), and the community working group developed interpretive content, a community profile, interpretive methods and program approaches, strategy, and implementation. Following each step, participants offered reflections and additional input. The board adopted the proposed strategic directions that shaped the final plan and implementation schedule that was completed by the fall of 2005. The inclusion of community representatives as equal partners to the scholars, stakeholders, and museum professionals was a transformative component of the mill's planning approach.

The early focus on community engagement allowed the mill to grow and professionalize at a fast rate. It opened doors to local resources, many new and dedicated volunteers, new avenues of financial support, and community partnerships. Following the interpretative planning process, the mill developed a plan for the production of flours and related products as an earned income stream. They hosted a Millers' Forum with other historical millers from around the country to discuss how professional standards for authenticity and millers' training could be established and maintained. The mill reached out to other regional museums, historic sites, and cultural organizations and worked with them to establish partnerships for marketing, joint promotion, and coordination of special events, such as hosting the regional farmer's market. The mill quickly established a reputation in the area as a community-friendly place, which helped to build attendance and attract new board members. This generated financial support, which helped the mill to add staff and complete the site's restoration.

Steps toward Community Engagement

Community engagement can begin as a part of a feasibility study, a strategic or master planning process, an interpretation and program planning process, a retooling for your organization, or an initial discovery process if your organization is new. In other words, there are many possible starting points. The goal is to incorporate community engagement into any and all planning that your organization undertakes, preferably at the beginning of the process, when public input can shape priorities and results.

1. Take a Leap of Faith

Community engagement requires a big leap of faith for some risk-aversive organizations. Especially at the beginning, the journey can be frightening as one cannot predict exactly where it will take the organization. However, after many years of working with cultural organizations on this transformative process, I can tell you with confidence that if your museum, historic site, or cultural organization commences a community engagement process with openness, honesty, and sincerity, the results will far exceed your expectations. Community engagement

opens doors, builds trust, connects your organization with new people and resources, builds awareness about your organization, and creates good will.

2. Examine Your Agenda

Before jumping in, it is critical to examine your internal agenda, or your organization's reasons for engaging the community. Initially, the motivation must
be focused outward, beyond your organization's specific purpose or mission.
The goal must be about building better communities or improving the lives of
the people in your community in some meaningful way. Since everyone benefits
from a stronger, healthier, more caring community, this goal will engage those
people who do not currently have a direct affiliation with, or interest in, your

Table 6.2. Steps toward Community Engagement

Take a Leap of Faith	Work through your fears. Begin it, even though you may not accurately predict the outcomes.
Examine Your Agenda	Your reasons for engaging community must go beyond your organization's purpose. Rather, focus on building a better community.
Make New Friends	Push beyond existing friends and stakeholders to establish new relationships with community groups and individuals. Put energy into a thoughtful selection process.
Plan Memorable Community Events	Even with very important work to do, community gatherings can be informal, thematic, and fun. Plan them as social events.
Ask What Your Community Really Cares About	Develop synergy by focusing on the distinctiveness of place and people. Help participants identify community assets, needs, and issues, and then envision collaborative solutions.
Work with Others to Implement New Ideas	Shift your organization from controlling and doing everything independently to working collaboratively for all activities and programs.
Articulate an Inspiring Vision	An inspiring vision can attract new board members, funding, partners, and community attention for activities. Articulate how your organization wants to change the world.
Develop Strategic Programs That Matter	Solicit ideas for collaborative programs that can help to address important community issues. Plan innovative program approaches with partner organizations.
Keep the Momentum Going	Share results of gatherings. Integrate community engagement into all activities. Form a community working group to participate in all planning.
Transform Organizational Operations and Practice	Work toward social entrepreneurship by paying it forward, giving back to those in need, and addressing social issues in your community, guided by the spirit and passions of your organization.

organization. Many community organizations, groups, neighborhoods, and individuals will thoughtfully participate because they support the larger goal.

3. Make New Friends

One of the underlying purposes of community engagement is to push beyond existing friends and stakeholders to establish new relationships with community groups and individuals, particularly those who are connected to networks of potential users and future target audiences. Hold initial conversations with community leaders and groups to introduce your organization and explain your reasons for wanting to interact with them. Ask for the community's help to identify who should participate. You may need the intercession of respected community leaders to engage members of their organizations. For large community gatherings, rather than issuing an open invitation to the entire community, purposively bring together people who can represent potential user groups and community interests. Include, but look beyond, existing members—for example, friends groups and representatives of educational institutions, such as teachers who have participated in past or current programs. Invite business leaders, clergy, youth group leaders, activity directors from assisted-living facilities, and representatives of neighborhood associations, clubs and social organizations, governmental agencies, and social service organizations. Include colleagues from other cultural organizations, tourism agencies, and hospitality businesses. Consider the current and future "movers and shakers" in the community and include those people who are already involved in important initiatives to improve the community.

The lesson here is to put time and energy into developing and using a thoughtful selection process and a very personal invitation process. This means carefully considering how your organization contacts people, and the more individualized and personal the better! The last thing you should do is issue a general letter or e-mail about a community gathering because recipients will perceive it as a mass communication rather than a personal invitation sent to the people you really want to participate. The outreach to potential participants will be much more effective if it occurs through an in-person visit or a phone call and is followed up with reminders from friends, acquaintances, or colleagues. This step is well worth the time and trouble because the outcomes of community engagement are directly related to getting the right people to participate.

4. Plan Memorable Community Events

Community engagement events have a serious and important purpose. However, these gatherings need not be formal (and potentially boring) occasions. Rather than calling and planning these events as "meetings" or "workshops," think about them as social events or gatherings with a seasonal or otherwise appropriate theme, decorations, food and beverages (preferably nonalcoholic), and a small thank-you gift for participants. Choose a neutral location that is familiar to participants—for example, a church hall or community center—as well as functional for an interactive session, with good lighting, tables, seating, a working kitchen, and a large open space. Do not hold these events in historic houses or galleries or spaces where furnishings cannot be moved or the walls cannot be used for posting materials produced during the gathering. Allow some time for socializing and networking before and after the gathering's working sessions. Make sure that events are organized and well facilitated so that when participants are working, their time and energy are used efficiently and effectively. Vary the types of activities between small- and large-group discussions and use the numerous techniques for gathering and sharing ideas; mix people up and keep things moving. Intersperse individual reflection and group dialogue. And if at all possible, make the evening enjoyable. When community engagement events are fun and memorable, they create a positive buzz in the community and attract additional people to join in future gatherings.

5. Ask What Your Community Really Cares About

One goal of gathering with community representatives is to articulate collectively what the community cares about, now and always. This is accomplished through carefully planned activities in which participants identify community assets, needs, and issues, then envision collaborative solutions. It is easy to develop synergy by focusing initially on the distinctiveness of place and people. For this step the community is the expert, and participants readily contribute their ideas and reflections. Once synergy is established, people are open to exploring how your organization can work with others to address what matters to the community. This knowledge can shape a new organizational identity and vision, as well as strategic directions, interpretive content, meaningful programs, marketing, and partnerships. Finding out what your community cares about is critical to shaping a more relevant role for your museum, historic site, or cultural organization.

6. Work with Others to Implement New Ideas

It is similarly important to make the shift from doing everything by yourself to working with others in the community for everything that your organization does. If your stakeholders continue to work by themselves, the input and wonderful ideas from community will feel overwhelming, pushing your colleagues to retreat into their patterns of autonomy and control. If this happens, your organization will move backward toward marginalization rather than forward toward relevancy.

Some readers may question this statement. However, it is a key understanding about community engagement. Once your organization goes down this road, there is no turning back. Engaging the community is not a one-time event. It is not a quick fix. It is a fundamentally different way of doing business that changes how your organization thinks and works, where and when your stakeholders interact with others in the community, and how organizational effectiveness is determined.

7. Articulate an Inspiring Vision

How does your organization want to change the world, or at least your community? Once community members feel that they have some context and background and a sense of organizational purpose, they can be very insightful in response to this question. Not only does their input provide fresh and often inspirational ideas for a vision statement, but their support, encouragement, excitement, and offers of collaboration can help organizational stakeholders to find the courage necessary to make it happen. An inspiring new vision can serve as a recruitment tool for new board members and a magnet for attracting community attention, new funding, and potential partners. When a vision articulates the organization's value and societal outcomes, addressing issues and needs far beyond organizational survival, it serves as an energizing force to motivate stakeholders to undertake new community roles ranging from facilitating dialogue to providing (with others) needed services. Perhaps most importantly, museums, historic sites, and cultural organizations learn that they share the vision of building a better community with many other organizations and groups.

8. Develop Strategic Programs That Matter

A new inspirational vision, one that expresses a deeper purpose shared with numerous other community organizations, provides a framework for bold strategic directions and innovative, collaborative programs. Public programs that address what the community cares about naturally attract new audiences, partners, and support, often from unexpected places. Hence, design a community engagement process that solicits ideas for collaborative programs that can help to address important community issues, including social, physical, psychological, economic, and spiritual needs. Articulate potential issue-related topics, innovative program approaches, and partner organizations that share an interest in the program's topics. Invite the potential partners to design and implement programs with your organization, with the goal of sharing the planning, staffing, other required resources, and results. Use the program planning process as an opportunity to make friends, learn about partner organizations' contributions to the community, and share what your organization is all about. The process must be a shared endeavor among all partners to be successful. Keep in mind that the emerging relationship is more important than the specific program outcomes because it represents the investment in building your organization's capacity. It lasts far longer than any exhibit, program, or event. Organizational research supports this collaborative approach because there is nothing more effective for building a productive relationship than working together toward a meaningful goal. This is also the quickest way to transform a group into an effective team.

9. Keep the Momentum Going

Once your organization has engaged a group of community representatives, it is essential to keep the momentum going by integrating this management approach into the ongoing operation of the museum. Here are a few examples of how to do this:

- Share the results of any community gatherings with all participants by preparing a summary of ideas, main points, and recommended actions. Ask for a follow-up reflection and continued input if community members have additional thoughts and recommendations.
- Publicize community engagement events in both internal venues, such as newsletters, annual reports, and social media, and external venues, such as newspaper articles and reports to community groups, funders, and governing agencies.
- Form a community working group comprising people who have participated in activities and demonstrated excitement and support for collaboration, new programs, new strategic directions, and working with your organization. The passion of potential working group members will emerge during community activities. Do not form this group based on credentials or positions of authority. Engage this group on a regular basis to provide input into organizational planning.
- Invite community participants to serve as new members of your organization's board and planning committees. This can be a particularly effective way to reenergize your stakeholders and quickly integrate community input into decision-making.
- Begin every planning process, be it for a strategic plan, a new program or event, a new facility, or an evaluation of existing programs and services, with a community engagement process. As this approach becomes an organizational norm, it facilitates the inclusion of a growing circle of community representatives and continually deepens your organization's relationship with community groups and organizations.

Do You Need to Hire a Consultant?

At this point, some readers may be wondering whether they can lead the community engagement process on their own or will need to enlist the help of a consultant to guide their journey. The answer depends on your organization's stage of development, stakeholders' skills (for example, facilitation experience), knowledge about your community, willingness to change, and level of courage. There is no question that strong leadership is a necessary ingredient for successful community engagement. For some organizations, the steps in this chapter will provide adequate guidance to begin the process and monitor its progress and to anchor the new approaches in organizational culture, strategic planning, and operational policies and procedures. Other organizations may find a consultant useful in getting the process started, with a pep talk that explains how the museum field is changing (refer back to the paradigm shifts at the beginning of the chapter), why community engagement is so important, why all stakeholders must be on board before beginning the process, and why it is beneficial to ask the community for help. Some museums need help in the planning and selection process in order to push beyond existing friends and stakeholders. A consultant or community representatives can provide this push, assuring that the right people participate in charting the museum's collaborative future role. Finally, some organizations benefit from a consultant's guidance throughout their journey because an experienced consultant can help stakeholders see the big picture and articulate the appropriate next steps. However, outside consultants, whether paid or volunteer, cannot ever lead this process by themselves. In all these scenarios, since we are talking about establishing and nurturing relationships with numerous community organizations, committed leadership from organizational stakeholders is necessary and critical for the long haul.

Boldly Changing Roles: Can Small Museums Become Social Entrepreneurs?

Social entrepreneurship, or social innovation, is a growing worldwide movement in which individuals, foundations, organizations from all sectors (business, public, and nonprofit), and the academy act as change agents. With bold social missions, social entrepreneurs are creating systemic sustainable improvements in society. When museums, historic sites, and cultural organizations engage their communities, discover what people care about (now and always), and transform their visions, programs, and services to address what matters, they move toward becoming social entrepreneurs. As new roles in the community emerge, ranging from facilitating dialogue about important civic issues to collaborating with other organizations to provide needed services, our organizations become change agents for building better communities.

Professor J. Gregory Dees of Duke University, in a 2001 article titled "The Meaning of Social Entrepreneurship," articulates that social entrepreneurs act as change agents by

- adopting a mission to create and sustain social value (not just private value);
- recognizing and relentlessly pursuing new opportunities to serve that mission;
- engaging in a process of continuous innovation, adaptation, and learning;
- acting boldly without being limited by resources currently in hand;
- exhibiting heightened accountability to the constituencies served and for the outcomes created.

These actions echo the broad paradigm shifts that I described at the beginning of this chapter about our mandate for meaningful public service: embracing interpretation, programs, and community engagement as everyone's business, and becoming learning organizations. So, while many museums initially consider it a big leap to move toward social entrepreneurship, it is happening, with rewarding results, as enlightened leaders realize that they must be more proactive in response to increasing societal needs.

Embracing Organizational Change and Transformation

In engaging communities and moving toward social activist roles, most museums, sites, and cultural organizations will undergo major change and transformation. As such, it is important to learn about the requirements and benefits of transformational leadership. Organizational research has shown that these leaders appeal to followers' higher values to build commitment to an inspirational purpose. They empower others to share leadership roles, and they demonstrate "serving and supporting" rather than "commanding and controlling" actions. There is more support for the effectiveness of transformational leadership than for any other leadership approach. However, it takes integrity and courage to do what is right for an organization, regardless of a leader's personal ambition.

It may also be useful for small museum stakeholders to understand more about the process of organizational transformation. It is a difficult, chaotic, and complex process that does not follow a simple, linear sequence of steps. Rather, it is usually a multifaceted unfolding of decisions, events, role changes, and redefinitions. Before change occurs, we must touch hearts and minds. Given this scenario, the importance of moving toward an inspiring vision of the future cannot be overstated—it is the lifeline that helps people come together and get through the chaos. William Bridges, a respected organizational change practitioner and author, notes that change leaders should focus on the transitions that people go through during the process of organizational change. Before embracing a new future, people must celebrate and then let go of past behavior patterns and organizational norms. They experience a chaotic "neutral zone" in which they try to understand why change is necessary and figure out how they will function in a new organizational reality. Transition is a wonderful time for organizational learning and collectively discovering how all in the enterprise can utilize their talents and skills to move the organization toward its envisioned future.

My research on organizational change in museums confirmed that meaningful participation helped stakeholders understand the reasons for change, built buy-in, and changed attitudes and behaviors. When meaningful participation did not occur, stakeholders resisted change, even if they thought it was a good thing. They also resisted change when they feared that they would lose control, power, competency, resources, or status. With this understanding in mind, it is important that leaders of museums, historic sites, and cultural organizations help people understand the process of change and how it will be implemented—particularly how it will affect existing roles, relationships, and responsibilities.

Especially in small museums where board members and staff often wear many hats and handle multiple functional responsibilities, it is helpful to remember during times of transformation that some activities may need to be postponed or discontinued. In light of moving the organization toward its future vision, it will be necessary to reevaluate and reprioritize existing programs, projects, and initiatives. If, for example, a community engagement process results in recommendations for existing museum programs or events to be collectively offered by a number of community partners, then it is necessary to transform how the new programs and events are conceptualized, planned, and implemented. The old way of working on these activities will no longer be effective. Similarly, if a small museum decides to undertake a capital campaign to improve facilities, staff and board must transform existing roles and responsibilities to accommodate this high-priority activity. It will be impossible to take on this enormous new task and maintain all other programs and activities.

Small museum boards need to model the transformation that they desire by becoming change agents, building support for change and organizational capacity, and becoming more effective governing bodies. Particularly in situations where the organization is transforming to focus outward and serve the community in more meaningful ways, board members need to partner with the director and staff to drive the transformation forward. They may need to take an active role in championing the transformation through securing new support and resources, reaching out to other community leaders, using their influence to open doors, and advocating for the organization in political arenas. Board members can help staff and outsiders to strategically understand the museum as a part of a larger community system. They can help the museum to shift its thinking and perspective away from short-term efficiency models and toward long-term effectiveness. If, however, the current board is not up to the task of transformation, then the first step is very clear: The board must change its membership and find people who are exited about the new vision and willing to work to make it happen. For some museums, historic sites, and cultural organizations, transforming the board may be the most important accomplishment in the journey toward becoming more relevant community organizations.

Summary

This chapter discussed why and how small museums, historic sites, and cultural organizations are transforming to address what matters in their communities and becoming more relevant and sustainable organizations. Within the context of some broad paradigm shifts that are occurring in the field, the challenge remains for museums to address what communities deeply care about. One could argue that small museums have a unique opportunity to undergo this type of transformation because they can draw on their existing community connections to deepen their relationships, find new friends, and use the input from the community to articulate an inspiring vision and shape a more meaningful future of public service. However, this will only occur if small museum leadership is willing to let go of old-school museum models, honestly listen to community ideas, discover what really matters to people, and realign their programs and services in response. The most enterprising small museums, historic sites, and cultural organizations will transform their organizational identities, priorities, and community roles toward becoming social entrepreneurs.

Resources for Further Reflection and Action

Bridges, William. *Managing Transitions: Making the Most of Change*. Reading, MA: Addison-Wesley Publishing, 1991.

Born, Paul. "Community Collaboration: A New Conversation." *Journal of Museum Education* 31, no. 1 (spring 2006): 7–14.

Borrup, Tom. *The Creative Community Builder's Handbook: How to Transform Communities Using Local Assets, Arts and Culture*. Saint Paul, MN: Fieldston Alliance, 2006.

Carbone, Sam. "The Dialogic Museum." *Muse* 31, no. 1 (winter 2003): 36–39.

Dees, J. Gregory. "The Meaning of Social Entrepreneurship." Center for the Advancement of Social Entrepreneurship. 1998, 2001. www.caseatduke.org/documents/dees_sedef.pdf (accessed May 30, 2011).

Florida, Richard. *The Rise of the Creative Class: And How It's Transforming Work, Leisure, Community and Everyday Life.* New York: Basic Books, 2002.

Hirzy, Ellen. "Mastering Civic Engagement: A Report from the American Association of Museums." In *Mastering Civic Engagement: A Challenge to Museums*, edited by American Association of Museums (AAM), 9–20. Washington DC: AAM, 2002.

Institute of Museum and Library Services (IMLS). *Museums, Libraries, and 21st Century Skills.* Washington, DC: IMLS, 2009.

Kouzes, James M., and Barry Z. Posner. *The Leadership Challenge: How to Get Extraordinary Things Done in Organizations.* 2nd ed. San Francisco, CA: Jossey-Bass, 1995.

Kretzmann, John P., John L. McKnight, Sarah Dobrowolski, and Deborah Puntenney. "Discovering Community Power: A Guide to Mobilizing Local Assets and Your Organization's Capacity." Evanston, IL: Asset-Based Community Development Institute, School of Education and Social Policy, Northwestern University, 2005. Available at www.abcdinstitute.org/docs/kelloggabcd.pdf (accessed May 31, 2011).

Matelic, Candace Tangorra. "Understanding Change and Transformation in History Organizations." *History News* 63, no. 2 (2008): 7–13.

———. *Organizational Change in History Museums.* PhD diss., State University of New York, Albany, 2007.

Matelic, Candace Tangorra, Donna K. Sack, and Beth S. Richards. "Giving Community a Meaningful Voice." *Proceedings of the ALHFAM Annual Meetings* 30 (2008): 115–19.

Pine, B. Joseph, II, and James H. Gilmore. *The Experience Economy.* Boston: Harvard Business School Press, 1999.

Shilling, Dan. *Civic Tourism: The Poetry and Politics of Place.* Prescott, AZ: Sharlot Hall Museum Press, 2007. Also see Shilling's website, with a wonderful annotated bibliography on civic tourism at http://civictourism.org/bibliography.html (accessed May 30, 2011).

Skramstad, Harold K. "An Agenda for American Museums in the Twenty-First Century." *Daedalus* (summer 1999): 109–28.

Tamarack: An Institute for Community Engagement. www.tamarackcommunity.ca (accessed May 30, 2011).

Weil, Stephen E. "New Words, Familiar Music: The Museum As Social Enterprise." In *Making Museums Matter* by Stephen E. Weil, 75–80. Washington, DC: Smithsonian Institution Press, 2002.

———. "Transformed from a Cemetery of Bric-a-Brac." In *Making Museums Matter* by Stephen E. Weil, 81–90. Washington, DC: Smithsonian Institution Press, 2002.

Worts, Douglas. "Measuring Museum Meaning: A Critical Assessment Framework." *Journal of Museum Education* 31, no. 1 (spring 2006): 41–49.

INDEX

defining, 144; demonstrating value to, 66; education, 86–87; festivals, *96*; geographical, 144; Howard County Historical Society policy for, 93; Kirtland Temple and, 76–79; leadership, 81–83; low-cost approaches to heightening role in, 80–81; measuring value to, 88–89; mission, 75; needs, 83–85; organizations, 81; universal center of, 95–96

community engagement, 142–43, *144*; Amherst Historical Society, 145–47; Burrows-Johnson on, 148; defined, 145; developing strategic programs, 156–57; events, 154–55; examining agenda, 153–54; examples, 145–52; Galt Museum and Archives, 147–48; Historic Germantown Preserved, 148–49; leadership, 158; leap of faith, 152–53; Mill at Anselma, 150–52; momentum of, 157; new friends, 154; publicizing, 157; South Dakota Agricultural Heritage Museum, 149–50; steps toward, 152–57, *153*; training, 146; vision and, 156; working with others to implement new ideas, 155–56

community service, 75–79; relationships and, 79–83

competitor analysis, 5–8

consultants: hiring, 158; Kirtland Temple, 91

Convention and Visitors Bureaus (CVBs): advertising, 15; mission, 7

cooperative advertising, 15–16; costs of, 16

cultural organization, 6

customer evangelists: cultivating, 4–5; discovering, 4–5; Internet and, 4; spotting, 5

customer service: sharing stories of, 132; understanding good, 121

CVBs. *See* Convention and Visitors Bureaus

deafness, 114

Dees, J. Gregory, 159

Delco Radio/Delphi, 68

Design for Accessibility: A Cultural Administrator's Handbook, 118

dialogic places, 142

Diamond, Judy, 43, 45, 58

Digg, 26

Distracted: The Erosion of Attention and the Coming Dark Age (Jackson), 125

Drayton Hall, 84–85

Durel, Anita Nowery, 82

Durel, John, 82

Dyer, Ellen, 94–95

Earley, Pete, 97n2

e-mail responses, 131

entrances, 131; accessibility, 108–10; Carnegie Museum of Montgomery County, 109–10

esteem, 122

Evans, Oliver, 151

evaluation: formative, 54–55; front-end, 54; remedial, 55; summative, 55

Everyone's Welcome (Salmen), 118

EXCHANGE, 118

exhibit accessibility, 110

Facebook, 26; advertising on, 29–30; Causes application, 29; General Lew Wallace Study & Museum fan page on, *29*; membership of, 28–30; nurturing relationships on, 31; responding politely on, 31

Falk, John, 123, 125, 126

focus groups, 43, 45–46; Howard County Historical Society, 68–69; pros and cons, 64

Follett House Museum: surveys at, 65–66; temporary signage at, *67*

"Freedom's Backyard," 148

Friesen, Steve, xii

165

ABOUT THE EDITORS

Cinnamon Catlin-Legutko has worked in the small museum world since 1994 and was the director of the General Lew Wallace Study & Museum in Crawfordsville, Indiana, from 2003 to 2009. In 2008, the museum was awarded the National Medal for Museum Service. Her contributions to the field include leadership of the AASLH Small Museums Committee, service as an IMLS grant reviewer and AAM MAP peer reviewer, and service as an AASLH Council member. She is now CEO of the Abbe Museum in Bar Harbor, Maine.

Stacy Klingler currently serves local history organizations as the assistant director of local history services at the Indiana Historical Society. She began her career in museums as the assistant director of two small museums, before becoming director of the Putnam County Museum in Greencastle, Indiana. She chairs the AASLH's Small Museums Committee (2008–2012) and attended the Seminar for Historical Administration in 2006. While she lives in the history field, her passion is encouraging a love of learning in any environment.

ABOUT THE CONTRIBUTORS

Kara Edie is a journalist and marketing professional who has served as the visitor services and marketing coordinator at the General Lew Wallace Study & Museum in Crawfordsville, Indiana, since 2004, specializing in emerging communication technologies. She also does freelance marketing, planning, and design work for nonprofit and for-profit industries. She happily lives in Linden, Indiana, with her husband John, her daughter Riley, and her son Jeremy.

Conny Graft is a consultant in interpretive planning and evaluation for museums, parks, and other nonprofit organizations. She is a faculty member with the Seminar for Historical Administration and has worked with clients such as the National Trust for Historic Preservation, the International Coalition for Sites of Conscience Immigration project, Drayton Hall, Monticello, and many other historic sites. She retired from the Colonial Williamsburg Foundation in 2010, where she worked for twenty-seven years as director of interpretive planning, director of interpretive education, and manager of research and evaluation.

Barbara B. Walden, born and raised in Southern California, received a bachelor's degree in history from Graceland University and a master's in museum studies from the Cooperstown Graduate Program. Her museum experience includes work at the National Baseball Hall of Fame and Museum, Women's Rights National Historical Park, and Kirtland Temple. Today, she is the executive director of the Community of Christ Historic Sites Foundation.

Kat Burkhart has a masters in anthropology and is a graduate of the Seminar for Historical Administration and the Institute for Cultural Entrepreneurship for Museum Leaders. She is the executive director/curator of the Carnegie Museum of Montgomery County in Crawfordsville, Indiana, and has worked in several small museums, including the Riverview at Hobson Grove (director) and the Astor House Museum and Clear Creek History Park (assistant curator). She was also president of the Association of Indiana Museums (2008–2010).

ABOUT THE CONTRIBUTORS

Tamara Hemmerlein was the director of the Montgomery County Cultural Foundation for thirteen years and the Montgomery County Historical Society for eight years. She is now the Hoosier Heritage Alliance coordinator at the Indiana Historical Society. She serves on the American Association of Museums Small Museum Administrators Committee and the American Association for State and Local History Professional Development Committee. She is a Museum Assessment Program peer reviewer and a graduate of the Seminar for Historical Administration.

Candace Tangorra Matelic, PhD, helps museums, historic sites, and cultural organizations to engage their communities as partners and then to fundamentally transform their visions, assumptions, organizational cultures, activities, and work patterns. Matelic has three decades of practical experience working in and with history organizations, as well as expertise in organizational change and development, transformational leadership, and strategic planning for interpretation and public programs. She is active as a teacher, planner, speaker, facilitator, and consultant and can be reached at www.transformorg.com.